"As a young strategic client service professional who's worked in both the United States and Australia, this book is my advertising bible. It's the real deal—if you are working in advertising and want to know how it all works, this is all you need to read."

Jess Norton
Integrated Account Manager
The Mark Agency
Canberra, Australia

"As a manager of a young client services team, this book is key. At IMPACT, we've made it a must-read for all of our new hires and it feels like we reference it daily."

Bob Ruffolo
Founder and CEO
IMPACT Branding & Design
\Wallingford, CT

"The Art of Client Service is the first book we give to new employees on how to approach account management. Robert takes what has become increasingly complex and translates it into actionable steps that help agencies get better at serving clients.

Drew Himel
Founder and CEO
PCR
Jacksonville, FL

"Over the years, I have handed out Robert's book as encouragement to account people who needed a bit of coaching. They always thanked me for taking an interest in their careers. Creative people found it equally insightful and wanted their own copies. With this new edition, I'll be advancing a lot more careers."

Richard Eber
Creative Guy
O2kl
New York, NY
Former Executive Creative Director
MRM

"Over the past decade, the discipline of account management has come under fire as never before. Externally, clients sometimes question its value, and internally, account managers fight to overcome the perception being order takers. The Art of Client Service shows how this critically important function can become more valuable than ever before, and how client service professionals can effectively evolve beyond the role of agency–client liaison to become proactive leaders of marketing initiatives. For years Robert Solomon's book has set the standard for developing a successful career in engagement management, and this new edition adds crucial new skills and principles needed to succeed in the twenty-first-century agency environment."

Tim Williams
Founder, Ignition Consulting Group
Author, Positioning for Professionals
Salt Lake City, UT

"Robert explains simply the complex issues of client relationship management with insight, practical advice, and humor—making it a must-read for all in the marketing communication profession and for anyone aspiring to demonstrate leadership. It's why it is required reading for all of my university students."

Sally Webster
Senior Lecturer
Public Relations and Organizational Communication
Victoria University
Melbourne, Australia

"The Art of Client Service is the first thing that people receive upon joining my team; it's the closest thing we account people have to a Bible."

Jamie Bryan
Executive Director, Client Services
Deep Focus
New York, NY

"As an agency owner, I continually seek inspiring, relevant resources to help motivate, train, and guide my team. Robert has a mastery of client service, and presents ideas not just theoretically, but in meaningful, actionable ways that directly impact our day-to-day business. The Art of Client Service is for anyone who values the often overlooked skill of developing, growing, and sustaining successful client relationships regardless of agency size or location."

Toni O'Berry
Principal
O'Berry | Collaborative
Bozeman, MT

"There are only a handful of books in my business library that seem to get better with age. Robert Solomon's The Art of Client Service is one of them. An instant classic when it was first released, Solomon continues to build on The Art of Client Service's usefulness, timeliness, and importance with each passing edition. It's a "must-read" for anyone involved in a client-facing business … and let's face it, we all are. If you are an advertising agency account manager or account executive, I highly recommend not only reading, but also living, everything in this book."

Ken Ohlemeyer
Senior Account Manager
Brighton Agency
St. Louis, MO

"For ad agency account managers, Solomon's book defines what it takes to be really great at the job. Great stories combined with relevant examples that go to the absolute heart of client service."

Roderick English
Marketing Communications Consultant
Adjunct Professor
Canisius College
Buffalo, NY

"Robert has crystallized for our industry a fundamental truth: that relationships of trust allow great work to flourish, but great work alone is never enough."

David Herrick
President, U.S.
Cohn & Wolfe
New York, NY

"The one constant in the constantly changing agency business, including digital, is **client service**. Robert Solomon has been the authority on client service for many years and The Art of Client Service has become a must-read for both newbies and veterans. His latest edition even includes a tactical primer that will make any agency professional just that much better."

David Vining
Vice President, Corporate Partnerships
CoreNet Global
Atlanta, GA

THE ART
OF CLIENT SERVICE

THE CLASSIC GUIDE
THIRD EDITION

ROBERT SOLOMON

Library of Congress Cataloging-in-Publication Data is on file:

9781119227823 (hbk)
9781119227939 (ePDF)
9781119228288 (epub)

Cover design: Belinda Downey, Color Colour Creative

Printed in the United States of America

10 9 8 7 6 5 4 3 2 1

You either get better or you get worse. So for me, I'm focused, in every way, on getting better.

Max Scherzer

**FOR MY PUBLISHING FRIEND DAN,
WHO TOLD ME THAT PUBLISHING A SECOND BOOK WOULD BE
HARDER THAN THE FIRST—A COMMENT THAT,
TO THIS DAY, REMAINS TRUE.**

**AND FOR MY WIFE,
ROBERTA,
MY PARTNER
IN ALL THINGS THAT MATTER,
INCLUDING THIS.**

CONTENTS

FOREWORD

Dear Robert,

When I started my advertising agency, Deep Focus, at the age of 26 in 2002, I had no idea what I was doing. What I wanted to do was reimagine the "agency" for a modern world with modern challenges, one unencumbered by legacy business models. As media changed around us, it began to change consumers, and I knew that clients would be met with more complex problems to solve, and more complex consumers to market to. One of the things I learned along the way was that businesses have problems to solve, and clients have problems to solve — and they are not always the same problems.

I thought the answer to building a client service–focused agency was just caring a lot about our clients' businesses. But it's so much more. If I had had *The Art of Client Service* by my side when I began, I have no doubt that I would have been able to accelerate the growth and maturation of our agency faster and more responsibly. We did a lot of great work in spite of not knowing how to properly manage our clients to greatness. We learned a lot of lessons the hard way.

But it didn't have to be like that. If I had a time-traveling DeLorean, I'd go back in time and leave a copy of *The Art of Client Service* on my desk.

I wish I had this book when I was starting out in my career, much less when I was starting Deep Focus. But I sure was glad a mentor gave it to me several years ago. Immediately upon putting it down, I made moves that fortified our client service organization, and enabled us to be able to not only weather the storm of an economic downturn, but emerge from it as an even stronger organization. It is now required reading for everyone on our client services team and beyond. In fact, I even recommend it to our clients so they can understand what to expect from their partners at Deep Focus—and why.

After building Deep Focus over the past 13 years into a global agency doing award-winning work for some of the best brands in the world with over 500 amazingly talented people, I've found that "client service" is something everyone who works here (including creatives) must take quite seriously. And great client service is what enables us to do the great work that makes us proud, and firing on all cylinders. It's why I encourage everyone who works at Deep Focus to read this book. It's why I have had you speak to my teams in multiple offices. And it's why I know my colleagues will benefit from reading *The Art of Client Service* from cover to cover.

Thankfully, as quickly as the world around us changes, that's how timeless *The Art of Client Service* is.

The rapid evolution of media and technology demands even more decision-making, more leadership, and more rigor from a profession that has historically been a great fit for generalists. But it's harder now to be a generalist than ever before because there is so much more to know, and so much more to do. And it's becoming more difficult to do all of those things simultaneously. Agencies need more training, development, and more hours in the day. Managing clients and agency teams has never been more difficult, and order must be brought to chaos to make sense of it all. If you're someone reading this, you're already well on your way to learning how to do just that.

The lessons you will learn from this book are supported by candid accounts and anecdotes that are relevant to you whether you're just starting out in this business or have been in it for decades, whether you run an agency or are just starting out as one. It will teach you how to be a leader, how to channel your empathy to motivate others, and how to guide clients toward great work, and how to build relationships that will keep on giving. Simply put, this book will help you be great at your job.

The new edition of this book features updated material, but still delivers the core concepts that will hold true as long as agencies and clients exist. It educates you about the mistakes many of us have made so you don't have to. And while many books about advertising are written about strategy and creativity, this one is utterly indispensable for anyone in client service. If you encounter a client management or service issue, you'll find solace and help in *The Art of Client Service*. If you're a manager, this book will be essential to helping you build a team of client service professionals who can enable great work, and a better business.

From time to time, I'll see someone reading this book in a train station, on the subway, or in a park. When I do, I give them my card. They've got their priorities straight, and I have a new recruit.

My sincerest thanks to you, Robert, for writing *The Art of Client Service*. This industry is better for it, my agency is better for it, and I am better for it.

Ian Schafer
Founder and Global Chairman
Deep Focus

INTRODUCTION

"IT SEEMS SO SIMPLE; WHY IS IT SO HARD?"

I didn't know Shelly Lazarus well; she introduced herself when I was running Foote, Cone & Belding's West Coast direct marketing operation and she was CEO of Ogilvy Direct, the direct marketing arm of famed advertising agency Ogilvy & Mather. Our paths would cross from time to time—we saw one another at a pitch for the Delta Air Lines' account—but we were far from friends.

Even so, after I wrote the second edition of *The Art of Client Service*, I sent the book to her. Shelly had by then ascended to become chair and CEO of Ogilvy's General agency; I was trying to generate some exposure and support for my newly published work. She was on the short list of agency executives to whom I planned to send a copy, with compliments.

I expected nothing in return, but Shelly was kind enough to write back with a handwritten note of thanks, which asked, "It seems so simple; why is it so hard?"

I have been thinking about this question for more than a dozen years. Serving clients well *should* be simple, except it isn't. Solving problems *should* be easy, but almost never is.

Very few people do these things well, and many do them poorly, which explains, in part, why so many accounts go into review, so many client people express profound unhappiness with their agencies, and so many agency people remain bewildered by a business that, if anything, grows more complex as people grow increasingly less able to deal with it.

The previous two editions of *The Art of Client Service* made a modest attempt to address this, deconstructing many of the things client service people need to do consistently well to serve clients effectively. The second edition was certainly an improvement over the first, but as helpful as it was intended to be, it had shortcomings.

Absent from that edition is any discussion about how to do something as fundamental as formulate a scope of work, a schedule, or a budget. New business, something utterly essential to the continuity and growth of advertising and marketing agencies, barely gets a passing nod. And ideas? They are the currency agencies trade in, yet hardly earn so much as a mention.

We need a book that preserves everything that worked in the previous edition, but also addresses these other, essential items, plus looks at client service in a way that is more accessible to account people, and potentially more effective with clients.

This, I hope, is that book.

I began by rethinking the book's organization, starting with what it means to be great with clients, the role account management plays in new business, and how client service people contribute to building and sustaining relationships built on trust. There's a section devoted to formulating a creative brief, and one that deals with unhappy clients.

Although the people I spoke with were far from a homogeneous lot—different agencies, different clients, different challenges—their issues were surprisingly similar and recurring, with five common threads populating the narratives I heard, all of which I share.

Everything begins and ends with *what clients want,* and what they want is relatively straightforward: consistent execution partnered with solid ideas, driven by people who understand and care deeply about their business.

Straightforward, but by no means easy. There is no bigger challenge than discerning, then delivering, near flawless performance in a business complicated with collapsing deadlines and compressed budgets.

Simply put, there are easier ways to make a living. But for those of us who believe in what we do, this is a calling, not a job, something we are committed to pursue as well as we are able.

If I've done my job even halfway well, what I've written will help you in your quest.

1

What Makes Great Client Service?

I was interviewing a candidate for an entry-level assistant account executive's position. She was fresh out of college; her work experience was limited to summer jobs and internships, but she was smart, aggressive, funny, and self-confident. For some reason that eluded me, she wanted to be an account person. I figured I might be working for her in 10 years.

After questioning this promising young person about everything from why she chose to study history in college to what she was currently reading, I asked if she had any questions for me. She replied, "I have only one." I figured she would ask me about the agency's goals, how I became such a self-important success, or something else grand and sweeping of that nature. But she surprised me.

"What makes a great account person?" she asked.

Simple question. Complicated answer. If you put this to 100 people in advertising, you would get 100 different answers. Here's what I told her:

It's more about skills and qualities than about education and experience. A degree in literature or philosophy might be more valuable than an MBA. Tending bar will teach you more than will working in a company that has no clue about collaboration or client service.

It used to be that agencies would train their account people extensively. These days that's increasingly rare. The training is shorter and less complete, and fewer agencies invest in it. But that doesn't place a set of handcuffs on you. Just because agencies don't teach doesn't mean you can't learn. You simply have to take greater responsibility for your own on-the-job training. Agencies offer plenty of opportunity for that, if you're willing to invest the time and effort. It might be between midnight and 8:00 A.M.; it might be on Saturday and Sunday. If you want to learn, that's just what it might take.

Speaking of nights and weekends, new business is one of the best places to learn. In new business, the agency moves at warp speed, ideas are rocket fuel, and some of the agency's smartest and most senior people inevitably are assigned to work on the pitch. Volunteer to help. You'll have to work nights and weekends on top of the nights and weekends you're already working. All you might get to do is fold, collate, and staple, but you will also get to observe. You will get to interact with senior people. You'll get to see them tackle a tough marketing challenge and how they solve it. If you're lucky, you'll get to participate in some small way in helping the agency win. You'll feel some of the heat that gets generated by one of these things.

Now what about skills? Communication is at the top of the list, both written and oral. You've got to be good on paper. An agency might teach you to write a conference report, a creative brief, a point-of-view letter, a strategy deck, or at least show you examples that you can use as "go-bys." What the agency won't teach, shouldn't have to teach, is concision and clarity, style and organization. These you must develop yourself. Start by reading William Strunk and E. B. White's The Elements of Style and William Zinsser's On Writing Well. Follow what they say and, no matter how good (or bad) your writing is, it will get better.

You also have to be good on your feet—in meetings, on the phone, in presentations, over dinner, or wherever else you connect with clients and colleagues. You can learn to be a competent presenter at an agency; you'll probably have the chance to present to your colleagues and your boss, if not your clients. If you work at it, if you practice, if you have an instinct for it, you just might become good enough to bring tears to the eyes of your audience.

No one is going to teach you to be good in the moment, to know what to say and just how to say it. No one is going to teach you what not to say, and when it's smart to hold your tongue.

Communicating isn't just about what you say; it's about listening and really hearing what the other person says. It's about the ability to interpret the subtext, not just the text, of any communication.

When it comes to skills, communication is the one every account executive must master.

There is one other skill that separates good account people from great account people: the ability to generate ideas. Many good account people have great integrity and solid judgment. They are masters of their discipline, communicate well, are good with clients, supportive of colleagues, and excellent at process. They may rise to very senior levels in their agencies, even to CEO. But if they are not idea generators, they fall short of being great.

Ideas are the blood and bone of advertising and marketing. Any competent agency can make an ad, but great agencies make ads fueled by invention, driven by ideas. Likewise, any competent account person can run a piece of business, but great account people can grow a piece of business by bringing ideas to clients that solve problems and capitalize on opportunities.

There are other things that matter—good quantitative and analytical capabilities, an orientation to organization and detail—but nothing matters more than the ability to communicate well and the ability to generate ideas. Ideas, and the ability to communicate them effectively, distinguish great account people from those who are merely good.

When it comes to qualities, there are two that stand above all others: integrity and judgment.

Integrity has always been an essential quality of the best account people; it is key to building trust with clients and colleagues. Judgment *is key to arriving at the right decision when the circumstances are less than completely clear.*

Account people need integrity and judgment in abundance to navigate what are increasingly complex issues and relationships that characterize the advertising and marketing communications business. The high-integrity account person takes ownership of problems. The high-judgment account person has the ability to resolve them fairly for all parties.

Great account people embody other qualities: patience, discipline, grace under pressure, a sense of humor, meticulousness, a sense of ownership, a spirit of collaboration, self-effacement, a sense of context, a service orientation. All of these are incredibly important.

Without patience, you have no hope of dealing with difficult clients and wayward colleagues.

Without discipline, you will never be able to focus on the task at hand.

Without grace under pressure, you will crumble under pressure. There is pressure in our business. At times it is intense.

Without a sense of humor, you will be unable to see that what we do is not brain surgery, and that we are not looking for a cure for cancer. We do advertising; it's critically important to our clients, but it is not a life-or-death matter.

Without meticulousness, you will make mistakes, and not catch the mistakes of others. An accumulation of small errors can undermine a client relationship.

Without a sense of ownership, you will not take full responsibility for delivering for your clients, and you will not step up when things go wrong. Your colleagues won't respect you, and your clients won't trust you.

Without a spirit of collaboration, you will be unable to marshal the full resources of the agency to the benefit of the client.

Without self-effacement, you will be dissatisfied with the lack of recognition account people receive.

Without a sense of context, you will see the details but not the larger purpose they serve.

Without a service orientation, you have no hope of helping your colleagues and clients achieve their goals.

With that, I paused. I wondered if the candidate sitting across from me was sorry she asked. No question I got a little carried away with my answer, but she seemed to still be with me. She was a good listener, and she was patient.

I concluded my monologue by saying that if I were to reduce this to four guiding principles, they would be integrity, judgment, communication, and ideas. Then I grabbed a piece of paper and drew this sketch:

"Does any of this make sense?" I asked.

"All of it," she replied. "Maybe I should be a copywriter."

I laughed. But she must have heard me, because today she holds a very senior, global role in an agency.

Part One

HOW TO BE GREAT WITH CLIENTS

2

Account Management's Role

Get a martini or two in me, ask me why my second marriage ended in failure, and I will say three words: "Lack of trust."

When I began in this business, I didn't give a damn about trust; I thought instead of the work. To me, and to the other people who shared my view, there is an unwavering belief that the only thing that really matters is the work.

Great work makes everyone want to be a part of the agency. Great work commands a price premium. Great work wins business.

If you do great work, everything else will take care of itself, including the relationships they build with clients. When I joined the advertising business as an account person, that's pretty much what I thought.

There's just one problem with this view: it's wrong.

Great work does not shield you or your agency from client loss. You can do great work and still get fired.

My former agency, Ammirati & Puris, did great work for BMW. The agency wrote the line, "The ultimate driving machine," which endures to this day. BMW kept the line, but they didn't keep the agency.

Ammirati & Puris is not alone. TBWA/Chiat Day did great work for Taco Bell. It's no longer Taco Bell's agency. Deutsch did great work for Ikea. It's no longer working with Ikea. BBDO did great work for Charles Schwab. It's no longer Schwab's agency.

You can make your own list. It will probably be longer than mine. So what went wrong? We know it wasn't the work. The work was great.

Then I thought about all the agencies whose work fell short of the mark yet somehow managed to hold on to the business. One of the best examples is Fallon and United Airlines.

After Fallon won the United business, it launched the "Rising" campaign. Wrong message, wrong time. People knew travel was hell; they were tired of the empty promises most airlines made. Yet the "Rising" ads clung to notions of romanticism that every savvy traveler knew to be false.

Not surprisingly, the campaign met uniform criticism. Fallon is a terrific agency, but this was bad advertising.

So bad, in fact, that you would think United would have gone searching for another agency. But they didn't. They stayed with Fallon until Fallon got it right.

Why was that? One report claimed that the close personal relationship between Pat Fallon and United's chairman kept the agency in good graces, even when its work was far from stellar.

What went right? We know that it wasn't the work.

I used to think that great work would lead to a great relationship. Now I think the opposite: a great relationship leads to great work. The reason is pretty simple.

Great work entails risk. Most clients do not want to take risks; they prefer a safe retreat into the world of the merely good or, worse, the dismissively average. Still, if they are going to take that risk, they are much more likely to do so with agency people they trust. And trust is the very foundation of a great relationship. And that's why I say a great relationship leads to great work.

Think of it as a perfect three-legged stool, or what my colleague Elizabeth Furze—she's managing partner at New York agency AKA—calls "the trust triangle":

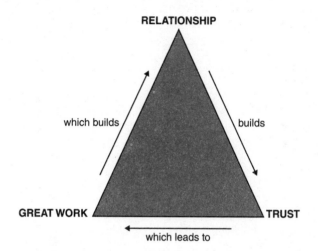

My colleague Tim Pantello says account people "need to be second best at everything they do," meaning they need to be nearly as good as the specialists in addressing client and colleague concerns.

It means your job, if you're in account management, is a bit harder and a whole lot more important than it used to be. There are no suits, no bag carriers, and no order takers. Instead, there are problem solvers, idea generators, and client-relationship builders.

As things grow more complex, with needs evolving and business mutating in ways impossible to predict, account management is not less important and marginal; it is more important and essential. Agencies need it, and colleagues—writers, art directors, planners, project managers, production people—depend on it. Clients demand it, and the reality is, you can't build great work without first building a great relationship with them.

Our mission must be to clearly define our role, execute better, communicate better, generate more ideas, and manage client expectations wisely, all the things outlined throughout this book. If we do these things well, we will build enduring, trust-based relationships with our clients. Relationships built on trust will lead to the best possible work. And that is what drives and inspires all of us every day.

3

Achieving the Next Level

What I know about opera pretty much begins with Maria Callas and ends with La Bohème, so it will come as no surprise I did not know Joyce DiDonato. Then I read Alex Ross's story about DiDonato in *The New Yorker*, and learned that she ranks among the world's most celebrated mezzo-sopranos.

Midway through the article, Ross quotes DiDonato:

"You know the four phases of an opera career? 'Who is Joyce DiDonato? Get me Joyce DiDonato! Get me someone like Joyce DiDonato! Who is Joyce DiDonato?'"

A native of Prairie Village, Kansas, a graduate of Wichita State University, DiDonato is about the furthest thing you could imagine in an opera star.

But it is not opera of which I wish to speak; instead, I'd like to talk about your career.

Most of us come pretty much from nowhere. Many of us fall into advertising. If we're reasonably good at what we do, there comes a time when someone—a recruiter, a colleague, perhaps a competitor—will say, "Get me (your name here)!" That's a happy moment, one that all of us would like to prolong for as long as possible.

How do we do this? And even more important, how do we sustain the "Get me you" for more than a moment?

Only a few of us will be smart enough to follow in the footsteps of a Shelly Lazarus or an Andrew Robertson, celebrated for their skill as client handlers. Few of us will have the courage of an Ivan Todorov, a John Hendricks, or an Ian Schafer, following an entrepreneurial spirit that drives the founding and leading of an agency.

Given most of us lack these skills, virtues, and vision, what are we to do?

If you work in client service, you are prized for being a generalist, for being, "A mile wide and an inch deep." You know a little about a lot of things; this is good. But to become an in-demand person—someone who others will say, "Get me so and so!" you need to become something else: a specialist.

For me, it meant becoming one of the go-to people in client service. I do workshops, I coach, and I consult around issues relating to forging enduring client relationships based on trust.

For you, it might mean becoming the go-to person in a discipline—direct response, retail, shopper marketing—a technology—digital, social, mobile, search—or in an industry—health care, financial services, luxury goods.

I don't know enough about opera to explain why people continue to say, "Get me Joyce DiDonato!" It could be, as writer Alex Ross explains, that *"She is literate in pop culture and adept at social media, yet is a classicist at heart, disciplined and tradition-minded."*

But DiDonato is a realist. She is all too aware there will come a time when people will say, "Who is Joyce DiDonato?"

I have no doubt that many of you are truly exceptional; even so, the "Who is" moment is likely to make a visit at some point. So, even as you cultivate yourself as an all-around, get-it-done person, think about what you are really good at, what drives you, what motivates you to excel, then pursue this with a commitment that will have others saying, for many years to come, "Get me you!"

When that day comes, it means you are on the verge of achieving the next level of our career.

4

Transforming a Career into a Calling

Charlie Rose interviewed the Princeton University professor, historian, and civil war author James McPherson about his latest book on Confederate President Jefferson Davis, but the conversation soon turned to a larger-than-life figure: President Abraham Lincoln. Rose asked, "How big was Lincoln's ego?" to which McPherson responded, "Lincoln did not have an ego problem at all; quite the opposite. He was quite ready to recognize that other people might know more than he did on certain questions. He was quite ready to take advice and to seek advice. He was thick-skinned about criticism.... Lincoln did not have this outsized sense of honor.... Lincoln was willing to work with his critics ..."

A lack of ego. A willingness to admit what he did not know. Open to the advice of others. Largely immune to criticism. Able to work with people who disagreed with him.

If I didn't know better, I would have thought McPherson was describing a truly extraordinary account person, not someone who unquestionably is among this country's greatest leaders of all time.

The qualities that define President Lincoln transcend personality, speaking to a deeper, more fundamental character. You don't necessarily need to be a great leader to be someone who aspires to, strives for, and ideally is defined by these qualities. You just need to be someone committed to delivering great client service.

If you are one of these people, I suspect you will find that you are pursuing much more than a job or even a career. You will find yourself devoted to a calling, a pursuit with its own reward.

Part Two

WINNING NEW BUSINESS
FOR YOUR AGENCY

5

New Business: What It Is, Why It Is Important, and Why You Should Give a Damn

The shop I once worked at, Ammirati & Puris, was started by three guys in the Delmonico Hotel, with one client, Burials at Sea (yes, it's true). A year in, on the verge of dissolution, Martin Puris traveled to Germany and returned home with a car account. The client was BMW; the car was the model 2002. Thirty-five years later, "The Ultimate Driving Machine" has ascended to tagline heaven, with the once-great-now-defunct Ammirati remembered with enormous respect and affection.

The point of the story: there isn't an agency on the planet that can afford to ignore the importance of new business. For some agencies, winning is literally a matter of survival.

If you work in an agency, you pretty much know what I am about to share with you. The fact is, the agency you're at didn't become the agency it is by failing at new business. You've won clients by being persuasive about strategy, by merchandising ideas that are compelling, and by articulating a work process that makes sense. If anything, what follows will serve more as confirmation, and less as revelation.

If, however, you are new to the business, some of what I share should be helpful.

Let's start with a definition. Even better, two definitions: (1) what new business is to an agency, and (2) what new business is to a client:

- **For an agency**, a new business "review" or "pitch" is the process of attracting a new client—in the form of a finite assignment or as a longer-term relationship—that helps an agency grow and, ideally, prosper, by creating a source of new work, new staff positions, and new, profitable revenue.

- **For a client**, new business can either be exhilarating—an opportunity to form a relationship that will help it grow and succeed—or a nightmare, with the need to replace an underperforming incumbent shop, requiring significant investment of time and resources to make the change, entailing considerable risk.

Why does a client put an account in review? There are three possible answers:

1. **For good reason**: A company that doesn't have an agency, decides it needs one, and seeks help; or, it launches a new product, service, or brand that needs support.

2. **For bad reason**: An incumbent agency underperforms—the work, the cost, the process, or the relationship falls short—and must be replaced.

3. **For no reason**: A company's leadership changes—a new CEO, CMO, or other senior marketing executive gets hired—and decides to make its mark by demonstrating change is under way, and calls a review, leading to a change of agencies.

We live in a "kill it and eat it" world, with many project-based clients, in which there is no guarantee of an ongoing relationship. We also live in a world in which clients choose agencies; agencies don't choose clients. With few exceptions, clients all but dictate the scope, duration, and value of the assignments they award.

If agencies are to survive, or, even better, thrive, they need to pursue new business as if their lives depend on it. Because it does. To do this, they need to gain greater control of new business, but not just responding to incoming opportunities, but rather by aggressively seeking clients that meet its criteria for scale, duration, and quality.

So how do you gain greater control of new business? Some clients oversee the new business process on their own. Others rely on search consultants—the people or firms that, for a fee, work with clients to identify the "right" agency—for assistance.

Like them, hate them, or be indifferent to them, search consultants are here to stay, and are a reality of the new business process. It pays to cultivate a relationship with them. At the very least, you want to get on their radar screens so the next time they are retained to conduct a search, your agency will at least have a shot at being included in the consultant's long list of candidates.

The 4A's—that's the American Association of Advertising Agencies—lists 21 firms on its site; all are small, with many operating as solo or one- or two-person practices. You can find a current list by following this link: https://www.aaaa.org/agency/ compensation/Documents/Agency%20Search%20Consultant %20List.pdf.

To initiate a search or to gather agency data, the consultants on this list rely on a standard Request for Information (RFI) form, which you can find by following this link: https:// www.aaaa.org/agency/compensation/management/Documents/ agency_questionnaire.pdf. It's relatively short—a little more than two pages, with 26 questions—and bordering on sane. The reality is, however, that not all clients use search consultants, and not all consultants and clients rely on this questionnaire. There are horror stories of RFIs issued by consultants and clients that run to scores, even hundreds, of pages.

If you get one of these RFI phone books, I have a suggestion: throw it away. The best decision an agency can make is to *not* pursue a potential account, especially one that distracts you from a true opportunity, one you have a reasonable chance of winning. The potential client that sends you an RFI request that runs to phone-book length is, by definition, not a true opportunity.

So let's say there is a true opportunity your agency wants to pursue. What's entailed in the new business process? An agency search can take days, weeks, or even months (yes, that's right, months!), and every review follows its own peculiar order, but for many clients seeking a new agency, there are 10 steps to follow:

1. Identify a **long list** of 10 to 12 potential agencies that appear to fit the client's needs.

2. Create and send out an **RFI**; many clients follow the four A's' guidelines on RFI format and content.

3. Receive and evaluate **RFI responses**.

4. Select a shorter list of six or seven **semifinalists**; visit each for a credentials presentation, or have them visit the client.

5. Narrow the list to three or four **finalists**; brief them on an assignment that usually (sadly) requires "spec" creative.

6. Ask for separate **compensation** proposals.

7. Hear finalist **presentations**.

8. Make a **choice**; **negotiate** a fee.

9. **Inform** the losers.

10. **Announce** the choice.

There is a saying, "There are no silver medals in the Olympics of new business." I liken the process to a political campaign in which there's a war of attrition being waged, designed to weed out the silver medalists and arrive at the winner (my apologies for mixing metaphors).

All of this is well and good, you might say, but why does this matter? Who needs new business? Why should I, or my agency, care?

The answer is best contained not in a theory, but in a story. And that story is about an agency called McGarry Bowen.

McGarry was founded in 2002 by three Young and Rubicam veterans: John McGarry, Gordon Bowen, and Stuart Owen. Cut to the present: the agency has more than 500 people, with offices in New York, Chicago, San Francisco, London, Sao Paulo, and Shanghai. In 2008, the firm was acquired by the agency holding company, Dentsu. In 2009, it was named *Advertising Age*'s "agency of the year." In 2011, it was named *ADWEEK*'s "agency of the year."

How did McGarry succeed? I could give you a long answer—it could easily fill a book—or a short one. Let's opt for short: McGarry succeeded because of new business. The agency won an account, added talent; won another account, added more talent; over time, it grew to the scale it has today.

You might not care about any of this, but if you think of new business as your paycheck, or as your next promotion, you should care, by quite a lot. And if you do care, it means:

- Stepping up, stepping outside your comfort zone, taking risks, doing what is beyond your "normal" scope.

- Contributing ideas.

- Being on call to help, whenever and wherever, for whatever is needed.

- Getting *all* the details right.... That power cord for the computer, that remote clicker to present with, that spare projector light bulb, just in case.

- Most important of all, taking ownership.

This is as much about an attitude as it is about any particular action.

New business is the soul of an agency. With it, an agency can grow, hiring new people, offering promotions and new responsibilities to staffers, rewarding stellar performers. Without it, an agency stagnates, withers, and, ultimately dies.

I know which agency I want to work at. I suspect you share my view.

6

How to Contribute Before, During, and After Pitch Day

True story: years ago, before I became an "agency person," I was a client, seeking an agency. I identified three, one of which was a firm called Stone & Adler.

Stone & Adler made a visit; they were enticingly good presenters, plus had some smart, engaging ideas to propose—things well beyond anything I ever anticipated—the best by far of the three competitors.

But they were sloppy. Their slides were marred with typos; their people were casual, offhand, and even dismissive. It was as if I was lucky they honored me with a presentation. I found the experience diminishing, just narrowly avoiding insult. They came across as less than professional.

The other agencies I met with also had good ideas, but lacked the attitude and the sloppiness. I went with one of the other shops.

You would think the best ideas inevitably win in new business. I wish this were true; the best ideas *should* win.

But they often don't.

Stone & Adler had great ideas. But so did everyone else. The fact is, great ideas are not enough; to win, you need great ideas and *something else*. What is that something? Is it a magical ingredient, which once injected into a presentation, guarantees success?

Actually, there are many "somethings," that in many cases cumulatively amount to the difference between winning and losing. These "somethings" are not about ideas; they are about all the *other* elements that comprise a successful pitch. I refer to them as "casting and choreography," which begin with pre-pitch activities and end with post-pitch follow-up.

At last count, there are 11 such items to which a committed new business person need pay heed. All of these are simple and easy to master, and yet, if you visit most agencies competing for new business, you will discover most of them are ignored. This suggests a problem for those shops, but an opportunity for your shop, and for you.

I'm going to walk you through these step by step. If you're an account person, especially someone new to the business, you want to pay close attention, because these are items that not only might make the difference between a win and a loss, they might make the difference in the trajectory of your career.

<hr>

PRE-PITCH PREP

Your goal is simply to not present to a stranger. Why?

Strangers get to say "No thanks."

Friends are much more likely to say, "Yes, let's proceed."

The thing you want to avoid at all costs is to walk into a new business presentation in which you meet the prospective client for the first time. The odds are stacked against you before you shake the first hand or utter the first word.

How do you avoid being a stranger to the prospective new client? That's easy. Suggest a face-to-face meeting.

Not to present, instead to learn—not so much about the prospective company (helpful, of course, but you have other avenues at your disposal to gain insight)—but about the person or people sitting across from you.

Why are they seeking an agency? What keeps them awake at night? What challenges do they want help with? Which competitors do they admire, and why?

Forward-thinking, prospective clients will welcome the opportunity to connect, and will make a point of visiting your shop, and those of your competitors, as part of the pitch process. They recognize the value of seeing agencies in their habitat, knowing it reveals insights about culture and collaboration, or a lack of them.

But not all clients are forward-thinking. If you can't get an in-person meeting, a conference call is the best fallback option. Either way, spend some time in advance to get ready, using this to craft a short, focused questionnaire—no more than 10 questions—that guides your discussion, demonstrates the depth of your preparation, and the quality of your thinking.

Have as many of these meetings or phone calls as you reasonably can, with as many people you identify as having a say in the decision. No, I don't mean frivolous, easily dismissed calls in which it's obvious you are simply trying to curry favor with the prospect. Yes, I mean meetings and calls in which you can engage thoughtfully and productively with the person across the table or on the other end of the line.

Your goal is, as well as you can, to know the people you are going to meet before walking into the room to present on pitch day.

PRESENTATION TIMING

I mean timing in two ways: (1) the order in which you will present; and (2) the length of your presentation.

On presentation order, assuming there are other firms competing for the assignment, you want to present first or last. Present first to establish what you might call the pitch standard.

Present last to make a lasting impression on the prospective clients. Is there a preference? If the choice were mine to make, I'd choose last, even in the unlikely event a firm preceding you actually is able to win before you get to your presentation day. Yes, this could happen, but I'd take that bet, and there are obvious advantages to being the last agency on stage.

Prospective clients see lots of presentations during the review process; they tend to blend together, with differences becoming fuzzy. Being last, and being best, gives you the best chance of making an impression, and earning a win.

What about presentation length? Prospective clients will tell you how much time you and your colleague are allotted to make your case. Plan to use no more than *half* the allotted time—yes, I mean 50 percent—with your formal remarks, meaning if you get 60 minutes, plan to present for 30; if you get 90 minutes, present for 45.

Your presentation will almost always be longer than you rehearsed. Commentary previously unrehearsed will mysteriously appear, lengthening your remarks. Clients ask questions, and you will want to build in time and techniques to facilitate and encourage those questions. Good questions lead to discussion, discussion leads to connection, and connection often results in a win.

Discussion takes time, which is why you want to take no more than half the allotted time to present. The last thing you want is a client impatiently pointing to their watch, indicating, "It's time to wrap up" as you rush to cover the key point you want to make.

THE DESIGN OF THE ROOM WHERE YOU'LL BE PRESENTING

Ideally you'll be presenting at your shop, which will give you control over the look and feel of the room. You can dress it any way you want, and can be as creative as the opportunity requires and your imagination dictates.

But more often than not, you'll be presenting at a location of the prospective client's choosing. It could be a neutral site, like a hotel meeting room, or it could be at the client's office.

Most agencies don't give location a second thought. They walk into a room minutes before their presentation, having to set up on the fly. But if you think about this for a minute, you'll quickly realize there are advantages to being able to scout a room in advance of presenting in it.

If the client agrees, arrange to send someone before your presentation date to video and photograph the room. If this isn't possible—the venue is out of town, logistics are difficult, the client can't or won't be bothered—at least try to have the client take and send photos to you. Absent that, even a written description—size, layout, lighting, presentation equipment, the best way to handle props—can be very helpful.

Even if advance scouting is possible, and especially if it isn't, you want to ask the client if you can arrive for a room setup at least an hour before you are scheduled to meet. This will give you enough time to set up and test your equipment, decide on seating, and have some time to relax and compose yourselves before going on stage.

All of this makes sense, but what if you or your colleagues walk into a room and discover a disaster-in-waiting? If you've presented at prospective client locations, you know how often a room is too large, too small, too light, or too dark, with no place to display work and AV equipment from the last century.

Now you know why it's a good thing you arrived an hour before the presentation to deal with these issues.

Some of this is within your control; some of it isn't.

If the room is too large, present from the middle of the space, with the clients arranged around you, closing as much distance as you can between you and your audience.

If the room is too small, use the resulting intimacy to your advantage: rather than standing to present, perhaps you remain seated. If space is really tight, have your colleagues cede space to the clients, remaining off to the sidelines until it's their turn to speak.

If the AV equipment is outmoded or too arcane to figure out, you'll be glad and relieved, that you brought your own gear, which actually is preferable, given its reliability and your familiarity with it.

ASSESSING CLIENT CULTURE

Prior to presentation day, you will likely be buried by facts, figures, and all sorts of other data about the prospective client organization. These items are helpful, but you need to look beyond them to things that are harder to measure and quantify.

Are these people who show up in suits and ties, or in shorts and flip-flops? Are they formal or casual in how they approach potential partners? Do they like to talk, or do they prefer to listen? Do they ask questions, or do they need to be prompted? Would they respond well to a touch of humor, or are they more comfortable playing things straight? Are they accessible and open, or inscrutable and remote, or somewhere in between?

The more you know about how your audience is likely to behave, the better equipped you will be to calibrate your performance to their expectations.

How do you discover a client's culture? There are two ways: (1) first, you observe; and (2) second, you find a client you like and respect, and ask the simple, obvious, but essential question: "So, what's it like to work at ABC corporation?"

The thing you want to avoid above all else is a performance that's a dud. The first impressions you make will stay with you long after the presentation ends. Be sure you make the right ones.

SEATING THE ROOM

This will seem all too obvious, but before your presentation, you want to get the *exact* names and precise titles of every client person who will attend the meeting. Why does this matter?

You need the names and titles so you can create an attendee list that includes all of them, and all of you. This is more than mere courtesy or a sign or respect, although it is both of these things. For everyone in the room this serves as a kind of cheat sheet, making it easier to recall and address individuals by names, rather than forcing people to awkwardly sidestep this.

You need to know who the attendees are in advance so you can begin committing them to memory before the presentation, which will allow you to smoothly and effortlessly refer to them by name. From the titles you can begin to infer who the decision-makers are, and can make certain you don't inadvertently offend someone in a position of authority.

If it is unclear who the decision-maker(s) is, ask for guidance. I've been in presentations in which the lead decision-makers did not reveal his or her position of authority, which led us to fumble where we sat this person and how we addressed his or her concerns.

You need to know who the attendees are in advance so you can determine if the decision-maker(s) is in the room. If the answer is yes, you can use this information to govern how you want to arrange seating for the presentation.

Speaking of seating, the last thing you want is to place your firm on one side of the table and the client on the other, creating an us-versus-them environment, which is not at all conducive to conversation and collaboration. Instead, you want your people interspersed with their people, paying attention to rank, meaning if a client C-level executive is a participant, you want to pair this person will someone equally senior from your firm.

WE COME BEARING GIFTS

We already know there will be a list of attendees at each participant's seat, on agency letterhead. To this you want to add a meeting agenda, also printed on agency letterhead. If you have a piece of swag—an agency-branded pen, a notebook or writing pad, anything else helpful and utilitarian—it should be added to each place. Swag serves not only as a token of appreciation, but also as a manifestation of your shop's brand. In a sea of competitors, you want to be remembered. Swag helps.

NO DEAD BODIES

Every participant you bring to the meeting should be a presenter. The last thing you want is someone in the room who lacks an active role. This means everyone you bring must be practiced, polished, and ready to deliver their lines calmly and with control, no small task.

If the presentation is short, you will need fewer people. If it is longer, it will be easier to divide responsibilities among a larger group.

Each room you present in makes its own demands on the presenter. Regardless, you want to avoid creating distance between you and your audience, meaning you should eliminate a podium or any other intervening impediment. If the room is large, present from the middle. If the room is small, find a comfortable corner to work from, or consider remaining seated.

Presenting is like a relay race; the hand-offs can be smooth and seamless, or someone can drop the baton. All of us prefer smooth and seamless, which means you have to practice transitioning from one speaker to the next. Some of this is about what you say; some of it is about what you do.

As one presenter completes his or her portion of the presentation, the next person picks up the thread with a voiceover that goes something like this: "Let me build on what Jane/John is saying." Or, "Thanks, Jane/John, what we're going to cover next is …" The key is to make the shift from one speaker to the next comfortable and expected, not awkward and uncertain. One person sits down and another comes forward. If there's a remote clicker to share, this gets passed silently and smoothly, with little effort.

This part seems easy, yet I have seen this screwed up dozens of times by otherwise capable and competent firms, mostly because no one thinks to rehearse this, when well they should.

YOUR PROPS

There's a moment in the movie *The Wolf of Wall Street* in which the actor Leonardo DiCaprio, playing the character—or should I say villain—Jordan Belfort, pulls out a pen, holds it in front of an individual in the audience, and says, "Sell me this pen." Putting aside for the moment the incredibly unsavory nature of the character DiCaprio is portraying, this is a riveting moment;

it speaks to the power of using a simple, accessible prop in an arresting way.

The point is that the right prop in the right hands is a powerful presentation moment.

These days, the prop of choice is a PowerPoint or InDesign presentation, but using it well requires some planning.

Unless you know exactly what will appear on the screen word for word, slide after slide—a nearly impossible task for most of us—you want to figure out a location that will allow you to maintain eye contact with your audience in front of you, while remaining in touch with what appears on your slides. The best way to address this is to use your laptop computer as a teleprompter. It carries what is on the screen behind you and allows you to address the audience without having to pivot to refer to the slides, making the interaction vastly more seamless and fluid. Most software versions include the current slide along with a preview slide, making it easy to know what comes next and plan for an appropriate voiceover.

Besides your presentation, what else might you share? If this were the *Mad Men* era, you'd likely be toting in large presentation boards to show work. But these days any work you share is likely to be embedded within an electronic presentation. The same is true of anything else that takes the form of a video.

Still, if you do have boards to present, be sure to have them in the order in which you will present them. The last thing you want to be doing is to fumble for the right thing to appear. And once you're done with an item, have a very clear idea of what you want to do with it: maybe you'll want to pass it around the room for closer examination or perhaps a discussion. Or maybe you simply want to place it on a ledge or pin it to a wall. The point is, you want to know in advance, not suddenly appear tentative or uncertain.

A whiteboard or an easel might prove useful, assuming you are adept at illustrating your points as you make them. Sure, it's so last century, but there is something incredibly engaging about doing this in front of the audience.

There might be a prop suggested by presentation content. There might be a product you refer to, or an item like Jordan

Belfort's pen you want to have with you, something that illustrates or advances your argument, all in the service of presentation theater that can transform your pitch into something far more dramatic, riveting, and memorable.

THAT QUESTION AGAIN?

A client asks a question; the agency stumbles, first for someone to speak, and then for an answer that is short, precise, and actually addresses the client's concern. So after the first person is done struggling to find the right response, another colleague interrupts, with these classic, kiss-of-death words: "What my colleague Jane/John *was trying* to say…" betraying an agency at odds with itself. The more people who feel compelled to add their two cents, the more likely the agency looks tentative, unprofessional, and confused.

No wonder so many pitches are lost in this moment.

How do you address this? That's easy. You rehearse.

First, you revisit what you're presenting with a critical eye, bringing in people who are *not* working on the pitch—people completely unfamiliar with what you're trying to communicate—who bring a fresh and often unexpected viewpoint to their queries.

Second, you capture every possible issue, point of clarification, challenge, objection—some large and significant, others small and irrelevant—that a client might raise.

Third, you match each question to a person who will respond. That person prepares in advance to provide an answer that makes sense and that all of you agree with. The last thing you want in a meeting are signs of discord that suggest you are not on the same page with your points of view.

Fourth, and last, you set a rule that no more than two people may respond to a question, and that each responder will be acutely aware of the time they are taking, not to rush their answer, but to respect that one question might lead to another and you want to be open to this.

Okay, so you invest the time to compile a detailed and nearly exhaustive list of questions, select appropriate responders, and rehearse the responses. You get to the meeting, and a client asks something that is not on your list. What do you do then?

What you *don't* do is scramble for an answer. Regardless of whom the question is directed at, you should look to the presentation leader—usually the most senior person in the room, sometimes the person running the pitch, occasionally someone all of you agree in advance would referee situations like this—for guidance. He or she will quickly and confidently field the question—there's no time to waste—and respond to it, or turn to his or her colleagues and say something like, "Jane/John, do you want to take this?" having the instinct to know who is best qualified to respond.

Suppose that person is you, and you think someone else is better qualified. You are allowed to pass the question on to a colleague, but only once, and you don't want to be scrambling for a responder, unless, of course, you want the client to conclude you don't have a clue on what to say.

Which, by the way, is okay. As long as this isn't the answer to every question, it's better to simply admit, "We don't know but we will find out and get back with an answer today," rather than fumbling a response.

If your shop does know the answer, at the end of your response, you turn to the person who asked the question, and say, "Did we address your concern?" You listen carefully to what he or she says to be sure you addressed the issue to his or her satisfaction.

Questions matter, which means you want to get really good at answering them. That takes practice, rehearsal, and game-day coordination.

Some agencies view questions as a bother. Smart agencies view questions as an opportunity. Some agencies give this scant attention, or even ignore questions altogether. Smart agencies pay proper attention to this portion of their preparation.

———

HAVE A CHECKLIST, CHECK IT THRICE

Why do you need one? Simple: you arrive at a meeting only to realize you left your computer power cord at home. Or the remote clicker. Or a spare light bulb to replace the one that your projector just blew.

No matter how thorough you are at presentation planning, rest assured that something will go wrong. A checklist allows you to catalog the seemingly limitless number of small details that need attending to, ensuring your presentation goes without a hitch.

You could create a checklist yourself, but allow me give you a head start:

- Computer
- Back-up computer
- Presentation(s) on a flash drive(s)
- Projector
- Power cord to hook up the projector to a computer
- Power cord for computer
- Two long extension cords
- Spare light bulb for projector
- Remote clicker to operate projector
- Second remote clicker (if you want to reduce hand-offs)
- Spare batteries for remote clicker
- Two-sided masking tape, push pins to mount items
- Sharpie pens, in various colors, to write on an easel or white board
- Presentation agenda on agency letterhead
- Presentation attendees on agency letterhead
- Agency branded notepads, pens, other branded items
- Enough business cards to hand one to each prospect in attendance

- Boards or other props you'll need for the presentation
- Sufficient copies of the leave-behind—bound copies, flash drives, or both—for every prospect in attendance, plus one or two "spares" in the event the prospect wishes to share the presentation with others
- Directions to the client location and to the hotel if pitch is out of town
- Other things we need:
    - _____
    - _____
    - _____
    - _____

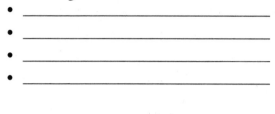

IT'S NOT OVER UNTIL IT'S OVER

Regardless of whether you hit the ball out of the park or went down swinging, you absolutely want to follow up.

Why, you ask?

For starters, what you say after the presentation is over says a good bit about the character and culture of your firm. Even if you did a less-than-stellar job, you want to do more than a cursory phone or email thank you.

You want to use your follow-up communication to correct what was wrong, clarify what was unclear, and connect on the reasons why you are the right choice for the prospective client, without even a hint of a hard sell.

At minimum, a thoughtful, well-crafted letter is in order. And in this case, I mean a real, ink-on-paper, signed letter—preferably delivered by courier or FedEx the day of or at the latest the day after the presentation—not merely an email. Ideally, it's written by the firm's CEO, who should be the most senior spokesperson available, addressed to all the client people who were in the room that day. If a key person was missing, you should customize your content, acknowledging that person's absence and filling in any blanks that occur as a result.

After one particular pitch, I recall that the team of presenters divided the room, with each of us addressing a follow-up letter to a counterpart. We didn't do one letter; we did a half-dozen. That was effective.

There are times when you will decide that a letter, or even a series of letters, is insufficient. You decide in that case to inject a bit of "showtime" into your follow-up. For example, there might be a theme in your meeting that you want to reinforce with your follow-up. Or it could be a comment one of the clients made that you see an opportunity to capitalize on. Or there is a way to further demonstrate how committed you are to earning the client's business.

I've seen situations in which a firm placed a very clever and appropriate follow-up communication on a billboard strategically located near the prospective client's offices. In another instance, I've seen a firm launch a customized microsite, directed at the client's needs and interests. And I've seen shops that quickly script, cast, and produce a follow-up video for web posting, again with the intent to reinforce a message delivered in the presentation.

The only way to ensure that any of this extracurricular post-presentation work has the desired impact is to be sure it appears immediately after the presentation. This means anticipating and planning for it *before* the presentation. If you wait to figure this out until the presentation is done, you might as well default to a smart, well-crafted letter—no small feat, by the way, given the time constraint—in lieu of something more ambitious.

Do any of these things actually work? They might; they might not. You invest in them if the opportunity is large enough or the odds of winning are long enough, to risk a kind of go-for-broke behavior.

The most important thing to keep in mind is you want to pay attention to follow-up, recognizing that doing it won't necessarily gain you the business, but not doing it will likely cost you it.

NO PHONING IT IN

The famed philosopher Woody Allen once said, "Eighty percent of success is showing up." That's how many marketing and advertising firms treat new business. They, in essence, just show up, hoping (and often expecting) to win.

That presents an opportunity. In the best of circumstances, new business presenting operates in a state of *organized,* controlled chaos. In the worst of circumstances, new business operates in a state of *complete* chaos. You want to reduce, if not eliminate, chaos.

Following these obvious, often overlooked, and incredibly simple details of presentation planning, then combining them with great people who deliver great ideas, ensures you will hold chaos at bay.

Pay heed to the details. Work to get them right. Assume nothing. Prepare for anything. If you do these things, and combine them with smart ideas and a polished presentation, new business wins will surely follow.

7

Getting to Yes

Maurice Levy, the chair and CEO of the French holding company Publicis, is reputed to have said about new business, "You never really know why you win; you never really know why you lose." I have no idea if Levy actually said this, but no matter. I believe it to be true.

I have been on the receiving end of many a condolence call from the prospective client that goes something like this: "You and your team were great, really great, and it was a hard, really, really hard decision, but we've decided to go in a different direction. But let's stay in touch."

And there have been a few occasions when I received this kind of call: "You and your team were great, really great, and it was a hard, really, really hard decision, but we've decided to go with you and your team. When can we get together to kick things off?"

The difference between winning and losing is often the thinnest of margins, and there are so many variables in play when you pursue a new client—money, the work, the people, the politics, did I say money—it is impossible to know exactly how you won or lost.

My agencies have done extraordinary work for prospective clients and lost. My agencies have done average work for prospective clients and won.

I had one prospective client tell me our agency didn't understand their business and that's why we lost. I had another prospective client tell me we understood their business so well that's why we won.

I once had a client visit our agency, listen to a credentials presentation, and make a decision on the spot to proceed. I had another client who never did make a decision, which means none of the competitors won.

In a new business effort in which there might be anywhere from three to 10 finalists, how do you avoid becoming one of the silver medalists? How do you walk off with that one gold medal?

With new business, there might be as many pieces of advice—some wise, others not so wise—as there are agencies, but I think there are three relatively simple rules to follow:

1. **Be ruthless about the accounts you pursue.** New business is all about handicapping risk. Smart agencies evaluate potential clients as carefully as clients evaluate them.

   You want to avoid the long shot opportunities and focus instead on those in which you have a reasonable chance to prevail. The key to winning is less about the accounts for which you decide to compete, and more about the accounts for which you decide *not* to compete.

   Do we really want this account? Can we help the clients achieve their goals? Do we like them? Will we get along? Is the money fair? Is the investment we need to make to win commensurate with the opportunity? How many other competitors are there? How do we measure up? Can we staff this properly? Will pursuing this account undermine the work we are doing for current clients?

   Questions like these help agencies reduce risk, increase the potential for reward, and help arrive at a decision to proceed, or, more likely, a decision to not proceed.

2. **Once you're in, go all out.** I am reminded of a player on a sports team who, in response to a question from a reporter, says that "We left everything on the field." The meaning is clear: that player and his teammates gave maximum effort, win or lose.

   If your agency is selective about the accounts and clients it chooses to pursue, it should be better able to devote the time, attention, and resources necessary to compete effectively. They follow every step included in the previous chapter. They leave everything on the field.

3. **Pay attention to relationships.** I was in a pitch once for a major financial services account. The agency I was working with was eliminated; the client chose another shop. But at the proverbial eleventh hour, a very senior client person stepped in and steered the account to an agency that also had been eliminated, proving once again that, in new business, relationships matter.

   It's easy to say the client's decision will be based on strategy, the ideas, and the work, and I know of no clients who willingly will admit to choosing an agency because they felt comfortable with the people they interacted with during the pitch process, but do not underestimate the power of personal connection.

Staying with the sports metaphor for a moment, if the score is close between your shop and a competitor, how the client feels about you and your colleagues could very well be the tiebreaker. You want to be on the winning side of that decision, and this means paying close attention to casting your team, and to taking all the necessary steps to close the gap between you and the client.

Getting to "yes" in new business is a little like shepherding a bill through the U.S. Congress. There are a thousand opportunities to veto something, but only one clear path to passage.

It's no wonder so little legislation becomes law, and why so few new business initiatives result in a win. I suppose many of us could take our marbles and go home but, for a few of us, that's the maddening beauty and wonder of advertising.

Part Three

BEGINNING A CLIENT RELATIONSHIP

8

In a High Tech World, Be Low Tech

"On the Internet, nobody knows you're a dog."

I was having lunch with two incredibly talented creative people when the subject of the new edition of this book came up. "It's been eight years since your last book, and so much has changed," one of them said. "Are you going to write about how to use technology to serve clients?"

I wasn't planning to write about technology. But then I realized that I have a cell phone, an iPhone, an iPad, a blog, a LinkedIn address, a Facebook page, and a Twitter account, along with an email address (very quaint) that allow me to be in nearly 24/7 contact with my clients. It's not at all uncommon for me to respond to client voicemails and emails at midnight. In fact, I make it a habit to respond within an hour or two of receiving something in my email inbox, and try to be equally diligent in responding to commentary that appears in social media.

So I figure I should talk about what having all this hardware and software means. I thought long and hard about it and ultimately came to this conclusion:

It means *almost* nothing to a good account person.

Yes, it's great to be in contact. Yes, it's both smart and productive to respond to voicemail and email at all hours of the day. And yes, your clients will no doubt approve of your dedication to their interests.

But there's something almost insidious about having this technology at your disposal. The client service people I know are busier than ever. The easiest thing is to email or late call. Get that task off your plate and move to the next one.

It's not just clients who feel the absence of in-person connection. Colleagues suffer too. Most agencies these days are arrayed in some form of open plan, with staffers sitting shoulder-to-shoulder, or at most with a simple partition separating workspaces. You would think it would be easy to turn to your left or right, or pop your head over a divider when you have a question to ask or a concern to share. Collaboration should be easy, except it's not. The people I've spoken with confess to preferring email or texting to speaking. Agencies remain strangers to themselves.

And therein lies the problem. As voicemail and email replace live, in-person contact, you find yourself in touch *more* but connected *less* with the people you serve. But advertising and marketing is about collaboration, of people working together. So in a business that is all about the twenty-first century when it comes to communicating, I urge you to remain firmly rooted in the twentieth.

I suggest you use technology to supplement, not supplant, the one thing that truly matters to clients and colleagues: face-to-face contact. Yes, meeting in-person is harder. Yes, it takes more time. And yes, it often is easier to phone or email it in. If you're skeptical, give yourself a month to meet with people rather than circumvent them through other means. Stick with it. Resist the siren call of technology.

There's a reason why people who rely on technology often refer to it as "working remotely." I couldn't describe it better, and it couldn't be more chilling.

9

What Success Looks Like

A client calls with an assignment. As usual, the deadline is tight. With no time to lose, you spring into action, gathering background material, organizing a team, developing a scope of work, a budget, a schedule, and any other item you need to brief a team and initiate work.

In that initial frenzy of activity, don't forget to ask your client, "What do you want this advertising to do?" It seems so obvious, and yet it's so easy to overlook.

You need to begin every client relationship, and every client advertising effort, with a clear understanding of what the client wants to achieve. Be sure to ask about the business goals, the sales goals, and the communication goals. Ask about the response the client wants from the key constituencies: customers, prospects, employees, company management, shareholders, the press, and the competition. How will the agency be evaluated? What will success look like, and can we accomplish it?

I'm all for clients having lofty aspirations, and for pushing agencies to achieve them, but you should encourage your clients to set goals that are in line with reality. On more than one occasion my clients have set objectives that were all but impossible to meet. A situation like this can turn success into failure, in which the problem isn't that the advertising fell short, but that the goal was too tall. This is something to discuss, and agree on, at the outset. This is not something you want to argue about after the fact.

When it comes to goal setting, you should pay attention not just to your clients' company goals, but also to their personal goals. Most of the clients I know are ambitious; they want to achieve success for their companies as well as advance in their careers. Usually the company and personal goals are aligned and mutually beneficial. Occasionally these goals are in conflict.

A client might be more concerned about protecting personal turf and power than collaborating with other departments to accomplish bigger and better things. A client might be so fearful of making a mistake, so intolerant of risk, that the agency is unable to do anything but average, safe work.

Personal agendas like these—sometimes hidden, sometimes quite apparent—can undermine your ability to do the best possible advertising. You must be aware of them, and take them into account when you sit down to define success at the start of a relationship or a project. It can be a balancing act, but remember that your first duty is to deliver on the clients' company goals.

I once went a little off course when it came to setting a goal for a particular ad campaign. My agency was creating some advertising for a client I knew well. I thought the advertising could achieve one result; he thought it could achieve a much higher result. In a moment of misplaced certitude, I offered to make a little wager on the outcome of the campaign. My client was a clotheshorse, so I suggested the loser take the winner to a certain very exclusive men's store and buy the winner one item of his choosing. With a smile and a laugh, he took the bet.

I was sure I would win, and figured I'd pick a pair of socks or something equally inexpensive. I didn't think my client had a prayer of winning.

It turns out the advertising achieved a result far greater than even my client predicted. A very happy problem to have. Because my client's estimate was much closer to being right than mine, it was time to take him shopping.

My client was very gracious. He could have picked a new suit. He could have picked a new coat. Instead, he chose a tie, and thereby let me off the hook. Every time I saw him in that tie, though, he would say, "Want to make a wager? I need a nice suit to go with this tie." It was our private joke.

There's no moral to this story except to say, define success at the outset, but don't bet on it.

10

Always Manage Client Expectations from the Outset

A creative director and I were presenting some concepts for a print ad to a client we really liked. Although this client had limited experience working with agencies and evaluating creative, he was smart, knew what he wanted, and respected our work.

We presented three ideas. The client responded positively to all of them, but was absolutely passionate about one particular approach, which relied on an illustration for the visual.

The creative director, who also was an art director, had done a little sketch of the idea he had in mind for the illustration. The client positively loved that sketch. "It's the perfect payoff to the headline," he said. "It's witty and charming." The creative director also had brought along examples of the work of the illustrator he wanted to use to execute the sketch. He showed the examples to the client.

The client wasn't wild about the illustrator, and he had a pained expression when we told him the cost. Still, he said, "You're the experts. If you say she's the right person to do the job, let's spend the money and go with her."

This story should have had a happy ending, but it did not. The client was bitterly disappointed with the finished ad. To him, something was lost in the translation between concept and execution. "This just doesn't work for me," he said. "It was great when you first showed it to me, but the finished ad just doesn't work as well as I thought it would."

It was especially painful to him that he had spent thousands of dollars on an illustration he didn't like. "I wish we had just used the sketch instead," he lamented.

I don't blame the illustrator; she executed the direction the creative director gave her. I don't blame the creative director; he thought he had buy-in from the client on both the concept and the choice of illustrator. He was mystified by the client's disappointment. I certainly don't blame the client, who was very supportive of what we were trying to deliver.

I blame me.

I did two things wrong: first, I missed the client's signals about his lack of full endorsement of the choice of illustrator and the associated cost. Second, I didn't manage the client's expectations about what the finished illustration would look like, and how it would differ from the creative director's sketch.

When the client hesitated about the illustrator, I should have said to the creative director, "Tony, can you explain how your sketch will translate into the finished visual?" After Tony explained, I should have turned to my client and said, "Are you okay with this? Have we been clear on how the illustration will *not* look like the sketch?" Had I initiated that conversation, had I drawn the client out, it would have revealed the client's concerns. Then, we either would have satisfied those concerns and managed the client's expectations, or we would have concluded we needed to find another way to transform the sketch into a finished illustration. We likely would have avoided the client's unhappiness.

That one incident had repercussions beyond the print ad. The client never again trusted us quite the way he once did. We had a harder time getting him to buy work from us. He became more risk averse. I'd even go so far as to say the quality of our work suffered.

That was a long time ago. These days, thanks to computer technology, agencies generally present initial creative concepts in such finished form they look like final ads. But the problem remains the same as before: if you don't manage the client's expectations satisfactorily, the client will take the concepts literally. Unless you explain otherwise, clients buy exactly what they see, which can limit the agency's ability to evolve the work to better place.

The lesson: manage your client's expectations from the outset. Make sure your clients understand how you and your colleagues approach a given assignment: what the steps are; what the agency will deliver at each step; when they will see the work and in what form; how to interpret the storyboard for broadcast or the comp for ink on paper or digital; who will present the work; and where you would like to conduct the meeting.

Listen carefully for client concerns, even when they are not stated overtly. Especially when they are *not* stated overtly. Ask questions. Probe for answers. Draw the client out.

I missed a subtle signal that, in retrospect, was quite clear. If you observe and listen to your client, you can do better than I did.

11

Be Multilingual

There's an old saying, "If the only tool you have is a hammer, every problem looks like a nail." For advertising agencies, the hammer has long been television, and it can make every problem look like one to be solved with a 30-second broadcast television spot. Sure, there's radio, print, outdoor, digital, social, and mobile, but the biggest tool by far in the agency toolbox is network television.

These days, network TV isn't quite the hammer it once was. First came cable. Then the web. In recent years we've seen the rise of social media and the power of mobile. Clients are investing more money in things decidedly not broadcast. They think less about advertising, and more about apps.

In a world of ever-expanding marketing choices and fragmenting markets, you need to be multilingual if you are going to provide your client good counsel. You've got to speak not only brand advertising, but also every other discipline and medium available to your clients. Given the number of options available, that can border on chaos. But that doesn't give you a pass. It still requires you to learn enough about each alternative so you can recommend the combination that will achieve the best results at the most efficient cost.

You don't need to become completely fluent in every marketing language. There are native speakers in every discipline and medium you can call on for help. The key is to be thinking about the best combination of marketing disciplines and media options to meet your client's needs, not about the next big TV campaign.

The advertising business refers to this as being discipline and media agnostic. I take a slightly different view. I call it being deeply religious—about mastering every facet of your craft, then delivering what's in your client's best interests.

12

Live the Client's Brand

Years ago, I worked for an agency that was one of three sharing a major financial services account. The client decided to consolidate its work with one shop, and invited all three incumbents to pitch for the business. I led the team representing my agency.

The shop I worked for was young, a little light on reputation, and very short on capabilities. We couldn't begin to equal the depth of resources of our competitors. The two other incumbents were bigger, better known, and better connected with the client.

We knew we were overmatched, but instead of being intimidated, we used our underdog status as motivation. We already knew the client's business, having worked on it for more than a year. But we acted as if we didn't, and went "back to school" on the whole industry. We dug deeply into issues and worked relentlessly to uncover insights that would help the client grow its business. We invested time in understanding what each person on the client team expected from its agency, and we made a strong final presentation.

To everyone's surprise, we were the client's choice. It was a big win for us.

Sometime later, after having gotten to know our lead client, I felt comfortable enough to ask him about the pitch and why we won. "All the agencies were good—any of the three could have done the job for us," he said. "What really impressed us about your shop was how you spoke our language. You sounded like one of us. You demonstrated that you knew what we were about. The other agencies didn't appear to be as comfortable or as confident. That made an impact."

It made an impact on me, too. It goes without saying that you should be a customer of your client. (If, as David Ogilvy has written, he found a way to buy all his clothes at Sears after his agency won that account, you too can find a way to use your clients' products and services.) But you need to go beyond that. You've got to steep yourself in the client's brand.

Here's what I mean:

- Know the history of the company. Know the people who work there. Observe the culture.

- Talk with other people who buy the brand. Ask them why.

- Read what the press says. Understand what Wall Street thinks. Pay attention to opinion leaders. Follow the discourse on social media.

- Form a point of view on the company and the brand's strengths, weaknesses, opportunities, and threats.

- Always be open to, and seek out, new sources of information and insight. Think about the new ways your client can address a problem or capitalize on an opportunity. Present those thoughts whenever appropriate and in whatever form and forum are most effective for your client.

At many companies, product and marketing managers come and go. When new clients arrive, their first instinct is often to put the account in review. Your years of knowledge can help counter that impulse. You can be an invaluable source of history and continuity for new clients. You can help them get up to speed quickly and be more effective in their jobs. In so doing, you can help keep the account right where it is, at your agency.

Just one more reason to live the client's brand.

13

Ask, "What Do My Colleagues Need to Create Great Advertising?" Then Deliver It

Years ago, for my first book, *Brain Surgery for Suits*, a creative director wrote this to me: "In my experience, account people spend too much time talking about partnership and not enough time practicing it. For your creative team, a detailed 16-point memo after the big presentation is no substitute for a lukewarm quart of Szechuan noodles the night before."

That creative director is right. Many account people think the best way to help your colleagues is to be a resource to them. That's important, but the best account people go beyond being the repository of market and competitive wisdom. They go beyond being the expert on client wishes, requirements, and idiosyncrasies. They are a constant, contributing presence on every assignment.

Here's an example: if the creative team is working late, or working the weekend to make a deadline, great account people will be there with them. They are there to answer questions, to provide input, to offer feedback and encouragement, and to order Chinese food or pizza. They are there in solidarity with their colleagues, participating and contributing to the process in any way helpful.

It is often the smallest gesture that makes the biggest impact. I remember a particularly stressful time preparing for a new business presentation. It was late on a Friday evening; most of the agency staff had called it a day. But one of my colleagues who was working on the pitch with me, a Planner, was struggling to make the final revisions to the creative brief. She wasn't the most proficient person at the keyboard. I volunteered to help.

We sat in my office and worked from her rough notes. She dictated; I keyed. In an hour we had input the revisions and had the final version ready for distribution to the creative team.

It wasn't a big thing; maybe I saved the Planner half an hour. But I know it made a difference, because the Planner thanked me more than once. To this day, we are friends, and on occasion she will remind me of that Friday evening. "You have no idea how important that was," she'll say. "You were a big help at a difficult moment."

She wasn't thanking me for my typing skills. She was thanking me for my gesture of support. It was almost as good as that quart of lukewarm Szechuan noodles the creative director was talking about.

By the way, I was at the agency early the following Saturday morning, to be available to the creative team. If I recall correctly, I brought bagels and coffee.

Part Four

HOW TO ...

14

Run a Meeting

"Could I please go back to the rack now?"

You might think this is an easy part, running a meeting, but then you quickly become acquainted with chaos.

Meetings that start late, with people who don't show up, people who show up but spend more time with their iPhones than with their colleagues. Meetings with too many people, too few people, or not the right people. Meetings without an agenda. Meetings with an agenda but no outcome. Meetings with an outcome but no follow-up. Meetings that devolve into shouting matches. Too many meetings.

I could go on. Meetings are a staple of business—including the advertising and marketing business, in which collaboration is key—but they are notoriously screwed up.

You can fix this, or at least give it a shot, by adhering to the five enormously simple, all-too-obvious suggestions that follow.

Start on time; end on time: Does anyone in advertising pay attention to this simple rule? I doubt it. Okay, with client meetings, agencies certainly try to be punctual. But then the clients often keep the agency waiting. If the problem is chronic with your clients, you have two options: (1) put up with it, or (2) gently, very gently, remind them they are paying for all those people cooling their heels in the conference room.

With internal meetings at the agency, everyone usually keeps everyone else waiting. You can do something about it, however. If it's your meeting, start it on time. If it's someone else's meeting, show up on time. If the meeting leader isn't there, or isn't ready to start, give him or her 10 minutes, then leave. Do that a couple of times and people will get the message.

With everyone on call to clients, there are going to be occasions when people will be late for internal meetings. The goal is to make that the exception, not the rule. The idea is to respect your colleagues' time, which allows you to ask for the same in return.

Once a meeting is under way, the goal should be to make it as short as possible. Get it done so everyone can get out and do the work.

Another secret to meetings that respect everyone's time is to have fewer of them. If people are chronically late to meetings, it might be the result of too many meetings that add too little value to the work process. So when you call a meeting, be certain it's necessary, invite only the people who need to be there, and make sure you accomplish what you set out to accomplish. If you do these things, you will become known as a person who gets things done. People might be late to other meetings, but they'll show up on time for yours.

Create an agenda in advance: An agenda helps you determine if you actually *need* a meeting, or if a phone call or an email will do. I'm a big believer in face-to-face contact, but I also know that too many meetings can impede work rather than advance it. That's the test: ask yourself if the meeting will advance the work. If the answer is no, or if the answer is that I can accomplish the same objective as effectively without a meeting, then don't have it.

Assuming the meeting is necessary, you should create an agenda, and not just in your head. Putting it on paper shows respect for the other participants. It also gives you a way to solicit input. This is particularly important when preparing for client meetings. You want your client's input before you get in the conference room. Nothing undermines efficiency worse than convening a group, only to find there is disagreement over the meeting's purpose and content.

At the meeting itself, the agenda provides focus, and helps keep you on course. Start by asking if everyone is comfortable with what's planned. If it's a client meeting, be particularly sensitive to the client's wishes. Restate the meeting duration: "This should take us about 30 minutes."

The agenda should be your guide, but don't let it control you—you should control it. Agendas are not written in stone, and agencies are in the idea business. If a meeting takes an unexpected but promising turn, be prepared to go with the flow. I've been in meetings when, quite unexpectedly, wonderful discoveries were made or insights revealed. In some of these situations, my agency colleagues and I were meeting on something quite unrelated to the breakthrough we achieved. Those are great meetings.

Come to the table prepared: I've been trapped in a thousand meetings and conversations that have gone twice as long as they needed to. I'm sure I've been as long-winded as the next person.

The way to shorten those meetings and conversations is to know what you want the outcome of the meeting, the conversation, or the presentation to be. Say what you have to say quickly, clearly, and concisely. Don't waste your clients' or colleagues' time. The workday is long enough as it is.

Above all, know when to close your briefcase. Once you have buy-in, it's time to move on. If you continue to talk, you might talk people out of what they just agreed to.

I know one CEO who can be very persuasive. He has just one flaw: he doesn't know when to shut up. He makes his case—people often agree with him—but then he keeps talking, and before long, those he persuaded are rethinking their decision.

You're probably wondering who that CEO is. It's me.

Guide the discussion: The objective is to keep everyone on track, and to ensure you efficiently accomplish what needs to get done, while leaving room for productive detours and digressions. You want to make sure all voices are heard, and actively seek participation from those who are more inclined to listen than contribute.

If anything is unclear, your job is to make sure it becomes clear by probing the other people in the room or on the phone. It's important to grasp not only the text of what people are saying, but also the unspoken subtext.

With clients, there will be times when you detect a subtext to a comment or a reaction, but choose to deal with it privately, after the meeting. You'll have to judge when this is the best course of action.

For example, if the subject of cost comes up in a large group meeting, it sometimes is better to take the conversation offline, where you and your client can speak privately.

Let's say you're in a large group meeting and you observe the client being short with one person on your agency team. It could be nothing, or it could be a sign of a bigger, deeper problem. You don't want to ignore the sign, but you certainly don't want to pursue it in a roomful of people. The right course of action is to follow up in private with your client.

In-person meetings are easy to run compared with teleconferences, but teleconferences are an unfortunate reality, especially with out-of-town colleagues or clients.

On the speakerphone, you don't have the advantage of face-to-face contact, or the clues of body language. Voice inflections become muddy. So you need to work extra hard to ensure that all views are expressed and heard. You must pay extra attention to hear the subtext of any client commentary.

Every meeting should have a well-defined ending, at which time you recap any decisions reached, next steps to be taken, and who owns them. This requires not only that you listen well, but also that you take careful notes.

In short, meetings matter. It's your responsibility to facilitate the desired outcome.

Follow up: Let's say I meet with a client to go over a creative brief or something similar. We discuss, negotiate, and agree. Or so I think. The next time we meet, I hear "That's not what we agreed to."

Sometimes I'm dealing with a client who suffers from a convenient form of memory loss, which seems to affect only his or her ability to recall our last discussion. Colleagues are not immune from the disease either, and I admit I myself have suffered from it on occasion. Other times, it's not a case of selective memory. Instead, something really did get lost in translation. You finish a discussion, you think you have consensus, only to discover there is a disconnect somewhere.

That's why it's critical to follow up every meeting, every call, and every decision. Never assume there is closure; secure closure. Immediately after the meeting concludes, follow up with an email conference report.

It is not necessary to revisit the discussion. Simply bullet the decisions reached and the next steps required.

You should do this for all meetings, but it is crucial for client meetings, because it provides an audit trail. Should a dispute arise later in the process, the conference reports or meeting notes will quickly confirm who agreed to what, and when.

Okay, here are those five suggestions again:

1. Start on time; end on time;
2. Create an agenda in advance;
3. Come to the table prepared;
4. Guide the discussion;
5. Follow up.

These suggestions won't solve the problem, but if you follow them consistently, I assure you things will get better, and you will become known as someone who really does know how to run a meeting.

15

Brief a Colleague

This is a book devoted mainly to serving clients well, so you might be wondering why I've included this chapter. Why bother with colleagues? Isn't this book called *The Art of **Client** Service*?

The answer is, you will never be able to deliver great work if you don't have team members who are as fully invested in a client's success as you are. And one of the keys to achieving this begins the moment a colleague—someone new to the agency, or an incumbent switching from one account to another—becomes part of the team you serve on. Hardly a day goes by without one agency colleague walking in the door while another walks out.

Add to this the reality that agency turnover was nearly epidemic before the financial meltdowns of 2001 and 2008, and the need becomes acute. The inescapable fact is new folks need to be briefed on that account you will work on together.

There are two ways to approach this. The first is to focus on the product. Useful, to be sure, but in reality, price-of-entry stuff. You're *expected* to know the client's products and services, and should be deft at analyzing, summarizing, and synthesizing them for your colleagues.

Product knowledge will take you just so far. Where you really earn your paycheck is with your knowledge of and insight into the client people you serve, and the corporate culture they operate within.

By all means spend time on the client's products or services. But be sure to then spend more time on how your client contacts behave, what they care about, how they interact with each other and with all of you.

What are your clients' hopes, dreams, and aspirations? How do they feel about the work you're doing? How do they feel about the process to get there? Have there been mistakes—there always are—that you need to address, and how did you address them? Are they open to breakfast, lunch, or dinner with the agency? Are there things outside the office they care about? Their kids, for example, or maybe sports. Do they have a hobby or passion they pursue?

On culture, what is it like to work at the company? Is it a morning place, an evening place, a weekend place, or all of the above? What are the politics like? Are competitive companies a threat, and if so, in what way? Do staffers believe in the product or service and its mission?

If you make a list of every client person you serve, identifying the things they care about, then adding key cultural components, I'm guessing you'll fill up more than a few pages with notes and observations. That's the point; that's how you truly add value.

Last suggestion: do your briefing as a conversation, several if needed, and not as a presentation. Most of your colleagues will tune out of a presentation, but a good conversation, preferably over lunch or a drink, maybe? Now you have their attention.

16

Write a
Conference Report

I remember returning home from a client meeting that was in a place called Mahwah, New Jersey. I know, you can't make up stuff like this. In a moment of snarkiness, we would say second prize was two trips to Mahwah. We didn't mean it—well, we did mean it, a little—but you have to admit Mahwah is as remote as it sounds.

In any event, my colleagues and I were back at our agency around 6:00 P.M. It had been a long, productive, information-laden session; the client was new, and I thought it might be impressive if I did a conference report that evening and had it on their desks when they arrived at their offices the next morning. So dutiful young account person that I was, I toiled late into the evening, converting my notes into a meeting recap that was, in fact, ready for client consumption the following morning.

The client was indeed impressed, and made a point of saying so. There was just one, minor matter: I hadn't written a conference report; I had written a meeting transcript.

A mistake made in earnest, I captured *all* of the meeting discourse—yes, as much as my furious note-taking scribbles would allow—making what should have been a relatively succinct document into something that went on page after page after interminable page, burying what was important in a swamp of needless, who-cares detail.

What I should have done, instead, is capture these four things: (1) the decisions reached; (2) the items outstanding still in need of resolution; (3) who is responsible for resolving them; and, (4) immediate next steps for both the agency and our clients to take.

A good conference report isn't long. It's short. It isn't detail laden. It is detail specific. It isn't comprehensive. It's concise. It shouldn't take hours to read. It should take minutes. And it shouldn't be a recap. It should be a plan-of-action.

The best way to describe a good conference report is to share one. What follows is a recap of a client conference call. It's addressed to the clients, with agency colleagues copied. It covers decisions reached, next steps, and who is to do what. It is as short and to the point as it could possibly be, without in any way sacrificing informality and friendliness:

Good afternoon Jodi, Allyson, and Kelly.

Many thanks for making time to speak today. I enjoyed the conversation, and look forward to meeting you in person.

In the meantime, here's a quick recap of next steps from today's call:

- *You will begin gathering and emailing Andrew the materials we requested in our December 16 Statement of Work. If we failed to include items you think will be helpful, please feel free to provide them in your data download. Among the items you'll send us are team bios.*

- *You will begin checking calendars to see what dates work for our two-day kickoff, which all of us agree should occur in February, after the contract is signed, which we expect will be next week, or the week thereafter at the latest.*

- *As part of the kickoff meeting, you will devote an hour or so to briefing us on the new product you are manufacturing that will be the subject of our direct response television advertising.*

- *You will check with your boss to see if it would be helpful for us to make a presentation on "DRTV 101"—likely to be an hour long—which all of us at the agency think will serve as helpful knowledge sharing, and as an effective conversation starter with key stakeholders.*

- *As part of our kickoff meeting, you will give thought as to who to schedule for one-hour one-to-one interviews to be conducted by the agency team, based on a questionnaire we prepare in advance and share with you for input.*

   That's pretty much everything on my list. If I missed or misunderstood anything, please let me know.
   Best,
   Robert

Most important of all, this recap went out really soon after we were done with our conversation. The call ended and within an hour—yes, one hour—I pressed "send" on the follow-up email.

The thing about conference reports is not only do they need to be clear, concise, succinct, and correct, they need to be fast. If they possess these qualities, it is more likely they will be read, confirmed, and acted on, and less likely to be gathering dust on a proverbial shelf somewhere.

17

Perfect the Perfect Scope of Work

Let's say you followed the advice I offered earlier and succeeded in winning a new client. The best part of winning is just that: winning. The hard part of winning is you now need to do the work that is a consequence of winning.

Assuming this didn't happen during the pitch process, one of the first tasks before you is to formulate a *scope of work* that articulates what your firm will provide, the time it will take, and the fee you will charge for your services.

Done well, a scope of work inaugurates a relationship in a positive and productive manner, affirming the choice your client made in selecting you, planting the seeds of trust you hope to nurture into a meaningful relationship.

Done poorly, a scope of work inaugurates a relationship in a negative and destructive manner, undermining the choice your client made in selecting you, planting the seeds of distrust you dread will plague you from the start, damaging or possibly even destroying any hope for a relationship based on trust.

One of the by-products of a poorly formulated and executed scope of work is something known as *scope creep*. What is scope creep, why does it happen, who does it happen to, and what can we do to reduce it?

Scope creep defined. This is going to be a bit longwinded; my apologies, but here's a definition:

You win a new account, or an existing client outlines a new assignment. You respond with a proposal. The client approves. You begin work. And then, mysteriously, the assignment grows in size, duration, complexity, or in some combination of the three. Your fee does not grow with it.

That's scope creep.

Why does scope creep happen? Most clients I know want to get as much service as they can for the least amount of money they can pay. No problem there, except when it leads clients to request work that *is out of scope*, meaning not accounted or budgeted for.

In their willingness to be flexible, or in the fear of losing an account, agencies give in to scope-creep demands all too often. The result—providing more and receiving less—encroaches the agency's bottom line.

To whom does scope creep happen? In a word: everyone. That's right, virtually *every* advertising and marketing services firm in the universe has to deal with the slow, steady, and often insidious incursions of scope creep. *No* organization is immune.

It's a lousy way to work, bad for everyone—the agency, its staffers, and, yes, even the client. Squeezed for revenue, agencies are forced to cut costs, which means fewer people doing more of the work, more junior staffing, and an unwillingness to invest. Agency staffers, overworked and undertrained, make an ever-increasing number of mistakes, or fail to deliver work that meets the level of quality expected. Clients, increasingly frustrated by work that falls short and a lack of good agency support, put the account into review.

This evolves into a *doom loop* for advertising and marketing services firms, is hugely damaging to the client/agency relationship, and, over time, does not serve the client's long-term best interests. In the end, *everyone* loses.

So what can we do to address this? What follows are eight ways to mitigate the influence of scope creep on your agency.

RULE NUMBER ONE: DO A SCOPE
OF WORK. YES, DO ONE!

You would be amazed at how many assignments begin with *no* scope of work in place. The client is rushed. The agency is too busy. The schedule is too tight. Work begins without truly defining what needs to be done. Fee estimates, assuming there are fee estimates, are essentially guesstimates that can be wildly off the mark. Clients don't know what's included and what's not. The result? Insanity.

You might think this doesn't need saying, but the first rule of business is to actually do a scope of work for *every* assignment, no matter how small it is, how tight the schedule, how demanding the client. The scope of work can be a three-paragraph email, as long as it accurately and fully describes the work to be performed, the time required to do it, and the amount of money it will take.

RULE NUMBER TWO: MAKE CERTAIN EACH
SCOPE FULLY AND PRECISELY DESCRIBES THE
TASKS YOU AND YOUR AGENCY ARE TO HANDLE

Lots of people do scopes of work, only to run into problems later. Why? Their scopes are lousy: incomplete, unclear, and needlessly vague. Instead of leading to clarity, they lead to confusion, questions, and general uncertainty about whether or not a particular task is in scope or out of scope.

You don't want to write scopes like these. Instead, you want to craft something that is detailed, meticulous, and abundantly clear. This means taking the time to thoroughly understand every aspect of an assignment, no matter how minor. It means consulting with your colleagues who will be collaborating on the assignment, to be sure nothing is overlooked. It means writing long, then editing for concision. And it means including a list of tasks your agency will execute to get the job done.

Here's an example of the type of list I'm talking about, on an actual scope of work formulated for a real client, addressing that client's repositioning needs.

A Summary of Tasks

Before I get to schedule and budget, I thought it would be helpful if I recapped the tasks we need to accomplish, and the deliverables that will result:

- *A positioning exploratory, leading to a final statement*
- *A name exploratory, leading to a final choice*
- *A creative brief, to guide all brand elements*
- *A logo exploratory, leading to a final choice*
- *A color palette exploratory, leading to a palette that will inform all brand elements*
- *First and second sheet letterhead, business cards, envelopes, note cards with envelopes*
- *Email signature*
- *PowerPoint template*
- *Website*

Each exploration listed above includes a minimum of three options, with up to three rounds of revision. If the items included here change, or if the number of revisions changes, we will revisit the fee estimate we included as part of our scope of work.

The list is a recap of everything the agency is expected to deliver, which, by implication, also suggests what is *not* included. If the client believes something is missing, it has an opportunity to address this with the agency *before* work begins.

———

RULE NUMBER THREE: IF YOU ARE UNABLE TO CLEARLY DEFINE THE WORK TO BE DONE, BUILD *CONTINGENCY DOLLARS* INTO YOUR FEE ESTIMATE TO DEAL WITH THE UNEXPECTED

Let's say you're working with a client on a fixed fee, project basis. The client calls with an assignment. You ask for details. What needs to be done? What are the tasks we need to execute? What's the timing?

Try as they might, your client is unable to address the questions to your satisfaction, making pricing more of a guess than a quote. You could make your proposal open-ended, but that's a blueprint for disaster, given neither you nor your client will know what the job will cost, ensuring a fight over money down the line. In situations like these, nobody wins.

You *really* want to price this as a fixed-fee assignment, but are at a loss. Okay, here's what you do: you accept the vagueness of the job, but price it according to the degree of uncertainty.

You build contingency dollars into your fee. The clearer you are on the scope of the job, the smaller the contingency amount, perhaps as little as 5 percent of your fixed fee. The less well-defined the job, the greater the contingency. The amount could easily escalate to 10 percent, 15 percent, or even 20 percent of your base fee.

It can help to think of this in visual terms:

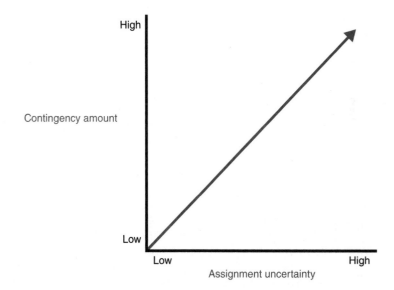

Contingency amounts can lessen the stress of executing an assignment without having to lose money on it. If the job goes better than expected, your profit margin will be higher. If the job goes awry, the built-in contingency fee provides the cushion you need.

Contingency dollars would be fine if you are competing for work in the absence of competitors. If only that were the case.

Your shop will often be up against other agencies, and in most cases, cost *will* be a factor in a client's decision. You don't want to price yourself out of an assignment.

My suggestion is you draw a chart like the one that follows. On the vertical axis, you think about client desirability in terms ranging from "I could take a pass" to "I really want this assignment." On the horizontal axis, you think about the competition in terms ranging from "There's little or no competition" to "The competitors are really formidable."

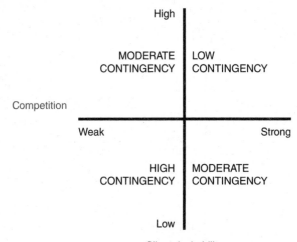

Client desirability

With this landscape mapped out, you have the context to decide how much, if any, contingency fee you want to include. If the assignment is one you want, and the competition is stiff, your contingency will live in the upper right-hand box and be low, perhaps as low as 5 percent, perhaps even as low as zero percent. You might go so far as to discount your fee.

If, conversely, you really don't want this assignment and the competition is weak, your contingency will live in the lower left-hand box and be high, perhaps as high as 15 percent or more.

If the job is desirable but the competition is weak, or the job is less desirable but the competition is strong, your contingency will live in the upper left- or lower right-hand boxes and be moderate, perhaps in the 10 percent range.

There's some science to this, but it's mostly art, as you navigate the murky waters of assignment uncertainty, with contingency fees as your compass.

———

RULE NUMBER FOUR: AVOID ADDING A DISCLOSED CONTINGENCY AMOUNT TO YOUR FEE

In the interests of transparency, and in the spirit of full disclosure, you could choose to make public that which you held private, by which I mean the amount of contingency fee you are charging your client. You create a line item in your proposal, decide the percentage of the fee you want to charge, and include it in your budget.

I am all for transparency, but let me see if I can describe what generally happens when you disclose a contingency amount to your fixed-fee proposal.

What happens is this: clients ignore it, or at least most of them do. They see your fixed-fee quote as a bottom-line absolute. They won't easily accept an automatic increase in your fee, and they surely won't give you license to charge it without justification beforehand.

All that contingency fee number achieves is client irritation at best, mistrust at worst. My suggestion: don't include it.

———

RULE NUMBER FIVE: INSTEAD OF A CONTINGENCY FEE, INCLUDE LANGUAGE THAT PROTECTS YOUR AGENCY

The best way to describe this is simply to share an example taken from one of my scopes of work:

Some Housekeeping Matters

All of the pricing I've quoted assumes a scope of work that closely aligns with what I've described. If the scope changes in any substantial way—in the type of work we perform, in the timing, in the number of revisions—the amount we charge will change with it.

I insert this language, or something similar to it, in every scope of work I issue. Does it eliminate scope creep? Sadly, no. But it does make explicit that a particular scope covers a specified amount of work, and if this work changes, the fee I quote changes with it.

RULE NUMBER SIX: WITH FIXED-FEE SCOPES OF WORK, BE SURE TO INCLUDE A CLAUSE THAT STIPULATES A 90-DAY FEE REVIEW

Even if you agree to execute an assignment for a particular fee amount, it doesn't necessarily mean you are held hostage to that fee. If you include in your scopes of work the point that you want to conduct a 90-day fee review, it will most likely limit your propensity to incur the assignment from hell, in which you grossly underestimate what you should charge and are now facing the consequences.

A 90-day fee review not only protects your interests, it also protects the interests of your client. This won't happen often, but there will be occasions when you didn't underestimate your fee; you instead overestimate it. If you find you are overcharging your client, and assuming you are open, honest, and honorable about what you charge clients, you will want to make an adjustment. A 90-day fee review gives you license to do this.

RULE NUMBER SEVEN: WITH RETAINER-BASED SCOPES OF WORK, BE SURE TO INCLUDE A MONTHLY FEE RECONCILIATION CLAUSE

Let's say you agree to a monthly retainer amount; a few months into the job you are wildly off the mark, doing far more or less work than you budgeted. Sure, if the work you're doing falls short of what you're charging, you could remain silent, collect the extra money, and hope no one notices.

The problem is, any halfway smart client *will* notice, and you will be forced to respond. Maybe you don't care about this client, but I assume you do, and for the benefit of the long-term relationship you hope to forge with these people, it is far better if you bring up the matter before they do.

Yes, you will be sacrificing some fee dollars in the short term, but the degree of trust you engender by being proactive and honest far outweigh the benefits of that extra fee, even if that fee amounts to a thousand, tens of thousands, or even hundreds of thousands of dollars.

The problem is potentially more disastrous if you are over budget rather than under. You are hemorrhaging money. The more time passes, the more money you lose. You could cut the service you provide, but that will make matters worse. Your client will notice the decline, grow frustrated, and ultimately be inclined to look elsewhere for help. Now, instead of losing money, you're losing an account. No one is happy with this outcome.

This is why it is crucial to always include a monthly fee reconciliation in your retainer-based scope of work. You want to be sure that the time you budgeted matches or is at least close to the amount you actually spend. And if it's not, you want to sit down face-to-face with your client to explore the reasons why.

There are an amazing number of reasons why the amount you budgeted does not match up to the amount you've spent. The scope could have grown. New, unanticipated assignments could have been added. The work is more complex than you anticipated. The timing is longer than planned. The number of revisions has grown beyond what you allowed for. All of these possibilities are symptoms of scope creep.

There are countless, logical reasons why things get screwed up. There also could be illogical reasons, such as a client who disregards the scope of work and what it includes and doesn't include, demanding instead that you and your agency do any and every marketing task that emerges.

It also could be that you (or the person who generated the budget) screwed up. You simply didn't understand the assignment well enough to quote on it and now are paying the price.

You can avoid all of this if you stipulate a monthly fee reconciliation, then candidly discuss the result with your client. If you are under budget, you can credit the client's account for future work, or add useful tasks that add value to the business. If you are over budget, you can discuss ways to get within budget, without sacrificing the relationship.

The fact is, a simple monthly budget reconciliation is the best way to keep a client a client, and to ensure you are paid fairly for the work you and your colleagues do.

Of all the rules you might want to adhere to, this is the one that is truly essential to your agency's well-being.

――――

RULE NUMBER EIGHT: MAKE YOUR LETTERS OF PROPOSAL SERVE AS YOUR SCOPES OF WORK

Many agencies I know do a letter of proposal, secure an assignment, then follow the letter with a scope of work. Why do this in two steps when you can do it in one?

Your letters of proposal *should* serve as your scope of work, for three reasons:

1. It saves time, and is vastly more efficient to create one document instead of two.

2. It forces vagueness and uncertainty to be expelled from your understanding of the assignment, allowing you to thoroughly describe the tasks you need to accomplish.

3. Letters of proposal customarily are written in the first person; scopes of work customarily are written in the third person. The "I/we/you/us" of a proposal letter is vastly more intimate than the "agency/client" language that besets a typical scope-of-work document.

Some people relish the option of a formal scope of work. I take the opposite view: I strongly prefer the informal, personal connection a scope-of-work letter of proposal offers. An informal approach can only serve to enhance the client relationship, which is everything you want to strive for, especially with a client new to your firm.

While we're on the subject of letters of proposal serving as scopes of work, let me also remind you this is the last place you want to introduce "Party of the first part" legal language into your scope of work vocabulary.

Why is this so important? The moment your scope even hints at the word *contract*—although that's what, in reality, it is—the lawyers get called in. Once attorneys are involved, you are more likely to finish the engagement before you finish the scope document. This is another good reason to keep your tone friendly, your language clear and accessible, and your intent—client approval—easily achievable.

Not too long ago I did a letter of proposal for an agency interested in conducting workshops for their staffers. After they gave me approval to proceed, one of the senior executives said, "I expect you'll want to send us a contract...."

I stopped her right there, with this: "I actually don't want to send you a contract, but I do want to send you an invoice. After years of doing workshops for lots of agencies, I learned that it is best to do a detailed scope of work in the form of a letter of proposal, and once that is approved, follow this with a bill. If we use the 'C word,' attorneys would need to get involved, and we'd be done with the assignment before we signed the contract."

To which my client agreed. An invoice followed. Attorneys sidestepped.

To summarize, here are these eight suggestions again:

1. *Always* do a scope of work, no matter how small the assignment or how time-pressed you and your colleagues are to deliver work.

2. Make sure each scope of work fully and precisely describes the tasks to be done.

3. If you are unable to clearly define the work to be done, build contingency dollars into your fee to help deal with the unexpected.

4. Avoid adding a disclosed contingency fee to your scopes of work.

5. Instead of a contingency fee, add language to your scopes of work that serve to protect the agency in the event the number, complexity, or scope of the assignment departs from what you have outlined.

6. Be sure to include a 90-day fee review in any scope of work for a fixed-fee assignment.

7. Include a monthly fee reconciliation for any ongoing, retainer-based scopes of work.

8. Make your letters of proposal also serve as your scopes of work, to help personalize your client communication.

You will never be able to rid yourself completely of scope creep, but if you follow these guidelines, scope creep *should* diminish. These items often are overlooked, but are surprisingly simple to execute.

Now all you need to do is execute them.

18

Craft That Schedule You Need to Create

When people ask me to describe *The Art of Client Service*, I say it is a book of *how*, as in, how to run a meeting, formulate a creative brief, develop a scope of work, and contribute to new business. I like that the book is practical, not theoretical, given that client service is about executing consistently and near flawlessly, day in, day out.

One of those *how*s has to do with figuring out a production schedule, something that often is included in a scope of work, but in many instances lives independent of it. Everyone should know how to do a schedule, right?

At some larger, more traditional agencies, this might be the domain of the traffic department, the project management group, or the production team. But in smaller agencies, and in shops that don't necessarily define themselves as agencies, so much of what gets done, gets done by account people, especially young, just-starting-out account people. People like some (or possibly many) of you. While I could assume everyone knows this stuff, I am going to assume some of you don't, and need help, which I am going to try to provide.

Before you begin to connect tasks with dates, let's start with a few observations and suggestions on schedules and their idiosyncrasies.

- **Not all schedules are created equally.** A schedule for a television spot is a world apart from website design, which in turn is a world apart from a print ad, which is a world apart from a social initiative. Each of these requires a different set of details.

- **Not every client is the same.** I know of no clients who say, "Sure, take as much time as you need with the assignment." That said, some assignments happen amazingly fast, others happen more sanely. So while the tasks remain the same, the time to accomplish each can vary substantially. In one schedule, for example, creative development might take as much as three weeks, or even three months; in another, it might take as little as three days, or even three hours.

- **It's helpful to outline not just tasks to be accomplished, but also who's responsible for accomplishing them.** This might seem like a no-brainer, but assigning a person or a team to each component of a schedule eliminates ambiguity and creates clarity. It also allows you to negotiate responsibility before you begin, rather than assigning blame—"I thought you were doing that"—after a ball gets dropped.

- **Start at the end.** This too seems pretty obvious to me, but the easiest way to build a schedule is to begin at the end, and work back. It's the most efficient way to determine where the time issues live.

- **Details matter.** I actually suggest creating two schedules: one, in great detail, for internal use; the other, an edited, shorter version, for your clients, highlighting key deliverable dates—yours, and most importantly, theirs.

- **Assume nothing, ask for everything.** Most people don't like a schedule imposed on them. Once you draft an early version, go see your colleagues in account, planning, creative, media, project management, production, and any other group whose help you will need. Tell them what you're thinking, expect a bit of back-and-forth, and try to gain buy-in. If you don't see eye to eye, negotiate something that works. You want to accomplish this *before* you present a schedule to a client, not after.

- **Understand the inherently unpredictable nature of the creative process.** Creative work is anything but linear. You do not progress from point A to point B to point eureka "I've got it!" Writers and art directors cannot mandate a creative solution. An idea can emerge in a minute, or in a month, and in some cases, never. You need to be acutely sensitive to this.

If you're looking for the typical minimum of three ideas to present to your client, don't give the creative team a day, or even less, to develop these. Instead, reserve enough time in the schedule to balance the need for speed with the need to deliver, knowing there will be back-and-forth discussion, with rethinks, rewrites, and revisions. Try to give the creative team as much time as you can afford, without pressuring the production people on their portion of the schedule, which comes later in the process.

The fact is, the business we're in—problem solving—is build-to-order, not build-to-stock, meaning every job is one-of-a-kind, and there are as many schedules as there are assignments. But here's an example of a highly compressed schedule for an actual television ad, starting with an approved creative brief, shot during the nearly impossible-to-produce Christmas holidays:

- Creative brief approved: 11/30
- Present three concepts to client; make selection: 12/4
- Final copy/concept and boards presented/approved: 12/7
- Award job to DP, Director: 12/8–9
- Casting and location recommendations/approval: 12/13, 11:00 A.M.

- Book talent: 12/15, 10:00 A.M.
- Pre-pro meeting: 12/15, 3:00–5:00 P.M.
- Final prep, wardrobe selection: 12/16
- Shoot spot: 12/17
- Finalize rough cut; ship to client: 12/22
- Client comments: 12/23
- Finalize rough cut: 1/5
- Final music, conform: 1/6
- Final conform/record and mix: 1/8
- Client approval for air: 1/9
- Ship for distribution: 1/9

Given how tight this is, with some tasks, we actually had to specify a time-of-day, not just a day. And knowing we had just a single day to shoot the spot, we conceived ideas that could be addressed in a single-day shoot.

Even so, this, by any measure, was tough to execute in five weeks, and required true client buy-in and commitment. Equally important, it required buy-in from creative and production, from the director, and from the production company we worked with. If any one entity said no, the spot would not have been produced as scheduled. Fortunately, everyone said yes, then went out and delivered as promised.

Sometimes things do work as planned. Amazing, isn't it?

19

Build a Better Budget

I'm not good at math. I nearly flunked algebra in high school. Forget calculus.

I never liked budgets much. I think of myself as a words person. No wonder there is nothing on the subject in the previous edition of *The Art of Client Service*.

But if you were to draw a four box grid, with the vertical axis that reads from "boring" at the top to "exciting" at the bottom, then follow this with a horizontal axis that reads "unimportant" in the left and "critically important" on the right, budget building would be in the upper right-hand quadrant, meaning "boring but critically important."

Formulating a budget ranks among the very *most important* but *least appreciated* or understood aspects of being in client service.

Let's say you do a budget that is well above the actual expense on an assignment. Money allocated for a project that doesn't get spent often winds up wasted; everybody loses. Your client concludes one of three things: (1) "These guys don't know what they're doing"; (2) "These guys clearly pad their budgets; I won't trust them in the future"; or (3) both.

Ever do a budget where the number you estimated comes in lower than the actual amount you spend, and, as a result, you have to ask the client for more money? How did that conversation go? I thought so.

Do a budget well, meaning a little above the actual expenditure, and your client is satisfied, your agency makes money, and you get to work another day.

Do a budget badly, meaning substantially off the mark—too high or too low—and your client mutinies, your agency loses its shirt, and you just might lose your job.

In the hope of sparing you the budget-meltdown grief I've suffered all these years, I am going to try my best to explain how I go about budget creation.

The expense part of a budget is relatively straightforward. For production, research, or any other major third-party cost, you usually turn to the specialists in your shop—mainly the planning, production, and media folks—for their input. If appropriate, you work with them on the specs, but then ask them to secure quotes from at least three bidders. They get the price estimates, analyze them, and present them, first to you, and then later with you to the client, along with a recommendation.

Agency fee—what your shop actually gets paid for the work it does—is an entirely different and potentially more complicated matter. This is serious stuff, especially when you consider that a client's fee payment is tantamount to your personal paycheck.

After years of doing thousands of budgets—yes, thousands—for scores of clients, I have realized that budgets are far less quantitative and vastly more intuitive than you might assume. It took me awhile to figure this out, though. Like most everyone else, I approached my first budget as if it were a math assignment. A very long, hard, and frustrating math assignment.

The agency where I got my start—you know it as Digitas—worked on a project basis, meaning each assignment needed its own budget for the time the agency would take to complete its work. I had no idea of how to do this, so I had to make it up.

This will require some patience on your part, but let me deconstruct how I went about this.

I would take each person in each department who would work on a given project and list their names down the left-hand side of a blank sheet of paper. Across the top, I would (attempt to) identify each task that each person would need to perform on that assignment.

Into this homemade spreadsheet I would insert my estimate — a guess, actually, since I had no clue — of hours and convert this to dollars by multiplying each person's hours by their hourly rate.

A quick digression here: everyone in our agency who was billable — from the beginners to the CEO — was assigned an hourly rate. It would seem this is a simple math exercise: divide a person's salary by the number of annual hours worked to arrive at a fee. To prevent anyone from figuring out someone's annual salary, we would place people in groups.

There was a "senior executive rate," which covered our C-level people and others highly ranked and paid accordingly. There would be a "middle-management rate," which clustered so-called mid-level people across departments. And there would be a "junior staff rate," which covered entry-level people and those with limited experience and titles to match.

There also were nonbillable people — in Accounting, Human Resources, Administration — who were not assigned an hourly billable rate. These staffers were placed into the agency's overhead factor, which was a percentage that we used as a multiple against our fee. The overhead factor included not only nonbillable staff, it also covered other forms of overhead expense, like rent, equipment, client entertaining, training, new business charges, and any other items that could not reasonably be billed to clients.

Figuring out the hourly rates was a simple exercise in math, once we settled on the projected number of hours worked each year.

How much time should we allot for vacation, sick leave, and holidays? How many hours in a day should a person work? How many weeks in a year should they work, taking into account vacation — two weeks, three weeks, four weeks — sick leave — five days, seven days, 10 days—and holidays? The higher the number of hours, the lower the hourly rate. The lower the number of hours, the higher the rate, possibly pricing a staffer out of the market in comparison with other shops. It's a balancing act, but that's why there are accounting and finance departments.

Assuming the accounting and finance folks make reasonable assumptions and arrive at hourly group rates, I work from those and total the figures by person and by task, and arrive at a final number of hours and an estimated fee. By dividing the estimated cost by the hours to be worked, I also could quote an average hourly rate, which clients generally expect.

I then would visit all the team members, show them the numbers, ask for buy-in to the fee hours estimate, or, if need be, negotiate a new number. Armed with only a calculator, every time I changed a figure to accommodate a complaint, I had to recalculate the spreadsheet. This was the pre-Excel era; my calculator became my new best friend. I felt more like an accountant, and a lot less like an account person.

Was this hard? Not at all. It was unimaginable torture. It took a day, or more, to create even the most modest budget.

But wait, it gets worse. I soon discovered there was no reality check on if I were right, or not right, in my assumptions. We had no mechanism for quickly comparing a *budgeted* fee to an *actual*, incurred fee. So why go through all the trouble of building a budget, task by task, person by person, if, in fact, there was no way to see if it was right?

Excellent point. I'm glad you're still with me. No matter how detailed your planning, it is all but useless unless you can check it against the actual expenditure. And yet the sad truth is, agencies are remarkably deficient when comparing budgeted numbers with actual numbers. If budget-to-actual comparisons are wanting, you should make it a priority to get this resolved, for the benefit of everyone's sanity.

Speaking of sanity, I knew I had to find a faster and easier way to formulate a budget. My solution actually was pretty simple. Instead of focusing on the tasks, I focused on the people. How much time—hours, days, and weeks—would each person need to complete the assignment? If it were a short-term project,

I would estimate the number of hours for its duration. If it were a longer-term relationship, I would estimate a percentage of time over the course of a year.

That simple insight was key. Budgets came together pretty quickly after that. And the more budgets I did, the better my instincts became.

But what really helped me was gaining a sense of not what a project would *cost*, but how much a client was willing to *spend*. I would run the numbers, arrive at a total, and ask, "Is this reasonable? Can I defend this to my client?"

The legacy standard was 15 percent of the total project cost, a holdover from the days when agencies charged a 15 percent commission on all media to be placed. That was a good starting point. The closer the number came to the magic 15 percent, the easier it was to sell.

But here's the problem: on smaller assignments with relatively little in the way of production or media cost, our fee would often be grossly out of line with the 15 percent "fair and reasonable" test. To convince a client of the rightness of our numbers, I needed to build a case for the time the agency would spend, then be prepared to walk a client through it in a face-to-face meeting, or failing that, over the phone.

I got pretty good at this, not just in doing my homework, but in reading the client. Some clients needed to extract a concession. Knowing I would have to negotiate, I built some financial room into my estimate. I could give ground without hurting my firm.

This also worked with clients notorious for scope creep, a challenge I discuss at some length in Chapter 17 of this book. We would agree on a scope only to see it grow after the fact. With these clients, I would anticipate the creep. To handle it, I built extra time and fee expense into the budget.

With a few clients, I knew I could trust my numbers, and would present them the way I calculated them. These were usually accepted without argument. (I love these clients. I just wish there were more of them.)

But what happened when we were at an impasse, when a client's figure and our estimate diverged? If the difference was small and the relationship was strong, I often would concede the numbers in the interest of investing for the long term. If the difference was large and the relationship was weak, I would look for ways to reduce the scope of work, thereby reducing the fee expense.

At these extremes, negotiation is always possible and the course of action reasonably evident. But many client relationships lack this black-and-white clarity. They live in the hard-to-read gray. In these cases, I would do my best to find a place where everyone was happy.

If this sounds confusing, it is because it is. I wish there were clearer answers; sadly, there aren't.

In the end, there are three takeaways about fee budgeting:

1. It's less about math, and more about intuition.

2. It's less about the tasks involved, and more about the people who perform them and the time they need to do so.

3. It's less about what you want to charge, and more about what your client is willing to pay.

But what if you don't want to get paid by what is essentially the hour? That's the point my friend Matt Neren, an Account Service Director at Denver-based Cultivator Advertising and Design, makes. His view: fees should not be based on hours. They should be based on value. Here's what he wrote to me:

> I propose a few more boxes for your checklist; many of these could probably be grouped under "intuition." We are a project-based shop, so my suggestions are biased to this philosophy.
>
> • What is the pricing precedent? If you charged $45K for a campaign last year, this is a good starting point for what to charge this year. Did the scope change with the new assignment? Was it painful last time?
>
> • What is the value of the project? We certainly honor "What your client is willing to pay," but that number is a factor of the value of the perceived value of the project. If it's important to them, they will probably be willing to pay more. If it's disposable marketing with a low potential ROI, they aren't going to want to pay a lot, regardless of how many hours are required to complete the project.

- *How many decision-makers are there? Projects with few decision-makers tend to get completed with fewer rounds of revisions and fewer problems. If your client's review process has a lot of levels, you will need to charge a lot more.*

- *How busy are you? If you are busy, charge more for projects, especially for new clients. If you are awarded the job, great. If not, fine.*

- *Let the staff do the estimates. As a partner in the firm, I sometimes underestimate projects. My staff has a better appreciation for the amount of work involved and often charge more because they are less optimistic about the assignment. I tend to think in context of the best case and my staff think about worst case.*

- *Break projects down into subprojects. If you turn a big project into a series of little projects, you have more opportunity to adjust your estimate as the project progresses.*

All of this is sound advice. If you're an account person seeking guidance on budget preparation, I suggest you add these points to what I wrote; it will help you navigate an often challenging numbers terrain.

Budgets are what keep clients awake at night. They should keep you awake too, at least until you figure out how to do them well.

20

Draft a Letter of Proposal

"*I just have a few minor fixes that will ruin everything you've come up with.*"

Writers get to fill their books with broadcast and print ads, some outdoor and web stuff, and maybe a collateral piece or two. Account people don't have books to showcase their work, but if they did, they would fill them with Word documents and PowerPoint presentations. Not exactly the most scintillating material, it's a better cure for insomnia than anything else. But the reality is if you want to be a really good account person, you need to master writing a good letter of proposal.

There are some terrific books on how to write well, and I include three in a postscript at the book's end, but I also think it would be helpful to explain five things that I think are critical in putting together an effective proposal letter.

1. **It's an agreement, not a contract.** I may be parsing words, but if you allow the lawyers—yours and the client's—to get involved in drafting a contract, the assignment will be over before you sign anything, and the only one to profit will be the attorneys.

   In all the years I've been in advertising, I have never needed help arriving at a client agreement. I've relied instead on a simple and thorough letter to establish an assignment's scope of work. Once I've completed the letter, I ask my client to sign it before beginning the assignment.

   Letters of proposal do in fact operate as legal agreements, but by keeping the writing personal and informal, I get to an outcome that's faster, cheaper, and better. And if you deliver on the scope of work you described, you won't need to call your attorney.

2. **Write the way you speak.** You are not trying to replicate "party of the first part" legal language. Write conversationally.

3. **Tell them what you are going to tell them.** After the usual pleasantries that you use to open the letter—"It was great to see you the other day, blah, blah, blah."—make sure

you outline what the rest of the letter will entail. The letter should include the following elements:

- A recap of the assignment
- A discussion of the various components you plan to include in the scope of work
- A budget estimate, both for your fees and any third-party costs you might incur (media, production, travel, and so forth)
- A schedule
- Next steps
- Another "thanks for the opportunity" closing, with a reminder that you will call to follow up

4. **Use short paragraphs.** Use headlines to separate the letter into digestible segments. Keep your paragraphs short; six lines maximum is the rule.

5. **Write it, then rewrite it.** The key to getting a letter of proposal that is clear and convincing lies not in the writing but in the rewriting. The editing process will not only sharpen your language, it also will clarify your thinking.

There are countless ways to write a letter of proposal, and I'm certain my approach is just one among many. Still, I thought it would be helpful if I included an example.

The letter that follows is one I sent to a founder of a firm. Everything I wrote is as I presented it, with the names of the founder, the firm, and its clients remaining anonymous, along with my fee estimate, for reasons of confidentiality.

With apologies to all the really good writers out there, here it is.

SOLOMON STRATEGIC

June 14, 2012

Ms. Jane Smith
Co-founder & CEO
ABC Company
1000 Any Street
Any City, XX 00000

Re: Letter of proposal

Dear Jane,

Many thanks for making time to speak last week; it was great to meet you by phone. I found our conversation illuminating and helpful, and hope we'll have an opportunity to meet in person next week.

In the meantime, let me begin this letter of proposal with a recap of our discussion and the challenge you and your partner face, followed by how I might assist you, the time the work will take, and the budget I propose to accomplish the tasks at hand.

A Recap of Our Discussion

By any measure, you and your partner have forged a remarkable partnership, characterized by its duration—26 years and counting—and distinguished by complementary skills sets. Your partner is an advertising executive of the traditional school, a savvy account person by training and inclination. You are known for your operational, get-it-done expertise, acknowledged for your administrative skills and digital know-how.

Together you have grown the agency to XX people, with a celebrated client list. People might not know the firm, but they surely know your clients.

What defines the firm is its ability to build enduring, trust-based relationships with the people you serve. With these clients, you tend to start small. Over time, the quality of your performance allows you to expand your portfolio, taking on new assignments or brands.

You and your partner essentially run the company as a two-person leadership team, but after 26 years, you have reached an inflection point. As you point out, you need to rethink your "infrastructure," and are in search of what you refer to as a "five-year growth plan." What resources do you need? What investments in staffing are required? How do we grow? What kind of clients do we want to pursue? Should we alter our methods of pursuit?

These questions clearly have a substantial strategic component to them, but let's be clear: execution is key. It is not just a matter of, "*What* should we do?" It is a matter of, "*How* should we do it?"

How I Can Help

There's a saying, "The best long-term strategy is a series of short-term strategies," that I think applies here. But another saying also applies: "The best way to predict the future is to invent it."

I cannot say with certainty what the firm will look like five years from now—there are simply too many variables in play to make precise predictions—but I am fairly confident we can craft a series of relatively short-term strategies that will help address the most pressing problems you and your partner are confronting, which will, in fact, help invent the agency's future.

What I am envisioning is a presentation that combines a strategic, detailed, and execution-oriented approach to new business development, combined with a thorough assessment of staffing needs that appreciates the realities of budget and the need to sustain profitability.

To best develop the plan, I need to spend time on the ground, at the agency, meeting with you and your partner, and with senior members of your team. I'd like to assess how you handle new business currently, identify what works, and what needs to be improved. I'd also like to revisit the agency's positioning to ensure it is meaningful, motivating, and differentiating to constituencies that include current and prospective clients, current staff and potential new hires, and the press.

Based on our conversation, my sense is that part of the solution we engage in might be staffing-oriented. There are any number of options to consider here.

For example, among the many roles you play, you serve as the de facto agency CFO and HR expert. I am not at all familiar with your current staffing situation, so I could be flat wrong about this, but to free up your time, we might consider identifying, recruiting, and retaining one or more candidates, either within the agency or outside of it, who ultimately could assume or ascend to a CFO or HR role, reporting to you, relieving you of these day-to-day operational demands.

We also might seek someone either within or outside the organization who could serve as head of new business development, which would be a key hire in your effort to achieve growth, knowing it is a priority to add to the three firms that reside on your current client roster.

Still another option would be to add someone in a more senior planning or strategy role, or to add someone who could serve as head of client service, both of which could add muscle to your firm, and possibly provide an assist to your partner in handling his day-to-day responsibilities.

Any one of these alternatives comes with a significant financial investment that must be weighed against the need you're facing. But the point is, I need to spend some time with you, your partner, and your team, to gain a sense of your strengths and weaknesses, to make an assessment, followed by proposing one or more possibilities for you to consider.

It also would be beneficial if I had an opportunity to speak privately with a few of your clients. Their perspective is particularly important, given they often reveal insights or make suggestions that might otherwise be overlooked.

Assuming we proceed, I would work with you to arrange anywhere from 5 to 10 client interviews. I would rely on a questionnaire I prepare in advance and share with you for input. The client meetings would take about an hour; if they are local, I would try to conduct them face to face. If they are out of town, or if time is an issue, I would conduct them over the phone.

The results would remain anonymous, but I would embed detailed client responses in the materials I present to you and your partner. This alone can prove to be enormously valuable as you think about how to realign the agency for the future.

We are tentatively scheduled to meet Thursday, June 28. Assuming we proceed with that meeting, and ultimately begin working together, I would want to follow up that meeting with three or four other on-site sessions, each a half-day or more in length, during which I can drill down on the specifics of your operation, observing the agency at work and asking the questions that can lead to insight.

Emerging from these internal and client-focused meetings would be a series of recommendations, delivered in presentation form, in which I suggest solutions and work through the issues. The ultimate outcome would be a plan that articulates a road map for you and your colleagues to execute. This would not be inflexible, "tablets etched in stone" output; rather, it would be a living, evolving document you can modify and update as circumstances change or opportunities arise.

How Long Will This Take?

I see you as being key to this process. Knowing you are to leave for vacation the week after next, I suggest we use the time while you are away for me to get up to speed on the presentations, recommendations, creative briefs, and other process documents that will familiarize me with the firm's operation, with a plan to schedule our first meeting late in the first week of your return, which would begin either the week of July 9 or July 23, given I'm traveling the week of July 16 and not be available that week.

We will follow this initial meeting with two or three others in the following two weeks. During these two weeks, we will schedule and conduct the client meetings, assuming clients are available.

It will then take me two weeks to prepare a draft plan for presentation to you. Figure a week for revisions.

The work will take six weeks to complete, but given I am out of pocket the week of July 16, let's make it seven weeks. If we start the week of July 9, we finish the week of August 27. If we start the week of July 23, we finish the week of September 3.

I should point out I am not someone who makes recommendations, then disappears. If there are matters with which I can continue to be helpful, I will surely propose them to you and your partner. But I also am mindful of cost, so my intent is to create something you, your partner, and the firm can choose to execute on your own, if you so desire.

How Much This Will Cost

Rather than propose this on an open, hourly or day-rate basis, I think it will be more cost-effective for you if I do this as a fixed-fee assignment, giving you a clear, certain cost figure regardless of the hours I invest.

I estimate it will take a total of X days over the six-week period for me to accomplish the tasks needed to arrive at a sound set of actionable recommendations. At my standard day rate, this would come to $_____.

If this is too rich an investment for you to make, let me propose an alternative: if the scope of work remains essentially as I've outlined it here, I will reduce my fee to $_____.

In terms of out-of-pocket expenses, I doubt there will be any, given I will cover the cost of travel to and from your offices. But should there be reason to travel, I will follow your travel guidelines, preparing an estimate for your approval in advance. I will invoice you at cost, with no markup or commission, with full backup documentation.

For any other expenses exceeding $100, I will secure advance approval. For expenses less than $100, I will again bill you at cost.

Next Steps

My sense is you and your partner have been thinking about the challenges involved in creating a five-year growth plan, and already have considered at least some of the possible steps you could take to address them. But you need a bit of a push, and this is where I can play a role.

I envision five benefits in having me collaborate with you and Art on forging a solution:

1. It forces both of you to **devote time** to think about various options, rather than postponing discussion while you attend to more immediate, pressing matters.

2. It provides an unbiased, **alternate point of view** to your own, which can further enhance your own thinking.

3. It potentially uncovers **areas of exploration** not previously considered.

4. It facilitates the creation of a **plan** you can put into place quickly and act on.

5. It adds another **pair of hands**—mine—to execute any of the items you agree to proceed with, but don't have the bandwidth to address.

I will follow up by phone later this week, to see if you have any questions or concerns I can address. But if you are comfortable with what I've proposed here, you can authorize me to begin work with a simple, "let's proceed" email. I will then issue an invoice that I bring to our meeting on June 28.

Regardless of the outcome, I enjoyed thinking about the challenges you face, would relish working with you, your partner, and your team on addressing them, and appreciate the opportunity to submit this letter of proposal.

Best,

Robert

Robert Solomon

You will of course develop your own style for writing letters such as these, but I'm hoping this gives you a start.

21

Create a PowerPoint Presentation

Much has changed since I last addressed the subject of Power-Point presentations in an *Art of Client Service* chapter called "The Zen of PowerPoint." It's not that what I wrote has become wrong; it's that PowerPoint has evolved to the point at which I'd like to suggest some new guidelines for you to consider, best told through a story.

Early on in a relationship with a new client, my colleagues and I were invited to present an introductory briefing on direct response television (DRTV) advertising to an audience largely unfamiliar with it. This would be our first time presenting to this client. It was an opportunity to make an impression. Or not make an impression. We were inclined to strive for the former and avoid the latter. Preparation of the presentation was in my hands.

I know a bit about DRTV, having spent the better part of my career as a direct response marketer, and I know that much of it—most of it, if I'm being honest—is junk, and discussion of it can be reduced to one word: boring. To avoid both, I figured I would need to do the following five things:

1. **Find a presentation title that transcends the obvious**. It would have been easy to give in and simply call this "An Introduction to DRTV" or something equally unimaginative. No way. The timing of the presentation was just before television's biggest advertising event: the NFL Super Bowl. My title:

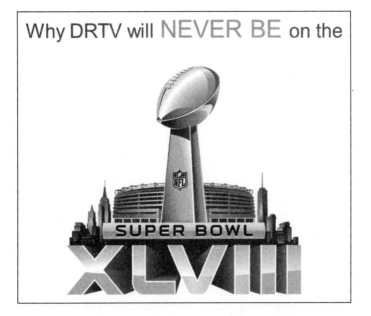

Why DRTV will NEVER BE on the
SUPER BOWL
XLVIII

   That was surely one step above the obvious, and injected a bit of humor into the proceeding. Even more important, it set up a construct that allowed me to explain all the reasons why a DRTV commercial will not appear on a Super Bowl telecast, and why this is a good thing, not a bad thing.

2. **Do *not* open with an agenda**. I know all the reasons why kicking off a meeting with an agenda makes sense, but the

moment you give in to this and start this way, all the theater leaves the room. I *wanted* a bit of theater, so I opted for what television programmers calls a "warm" opening. The title actually suggested an opening; I needed to introduce the session with a warm up that sets up the title reveal, which I did.

3. **Avoid bulleted copy**. Even eight years ago, I said, "My slides work like billboards, cuing me to the right content, helping the audience to follow along." In this age of TED presentations (for those of you who don't know, TED is an acronym for Technology, Education, Design), bullets are pariahs, to be forever banished from presentations.

4. **Be visual.** It used to be that people would populate their slides with bullet after bullet of mind-numbing copy. No more. The best presenters use visuals to make their point, supported with a minimum of copy. The examples that follow make this point:

The scale of the full-bleed images injects power into the message, helping to drive home the point I am trying to make. The word content goes on longer than it should. If I were being truly ruthless, the first slide would have said, "Super Bowl advertisers care about VIEWERS," and the second slide would have said, "DRTV advertisers care about BUYERS." But I lacked the confidence needed to trust the balance of the commentary to a voiceover, so I defaulted to longer copy.

5. **Think long and hard about whether you need to use a template**. For many of my presentations, I do rely on one that is designed to reinforce my company branding. The examples that follow are taken from another presentation I give:

We don't have the benefit of color here, but if we did, you would see that both slides are designed in black and red, the two colors that figure prominently and consistently in the Solomon Strategic brand. The background of the first slide functions as a kind of wallpaper—a placeholder—that's up on the screen when participants file into the room. The second is what I use to reveal the topic of the day's workshop. Both also make use of "Urban Headgear"—okay, it's a baseball cap, but I like the archness of headgear—that also figure prominently in the Solomon Strategic brand.

I confess to being ambivalent about relying on a template. On one hand, it can be far more powerful if each individual slide in a presentation is crafted to deliver a message without resorting to a template. On the other hand, the realities of time and cost make using a template far more efficient and cost-effective. None of us ever have enough time, making the use of a template a practical reality.

There are a fair number of books on how to make effective use of PowerPoint—Garr Reynolds's *Presentation Zen* is among the best known—but the point to remember is, badly used, Power-Point can eviscerate even the most thoughtful content. If you're going to use it, remember it's a prop to support what you say, not a replacement for what you say.

The DRTV presentation succeeded, in part, because it combined an effective oral presentation with a clever title, an effective warm opening, the intentional exclusion of bulleted material, the intentional inclusion of dramatic, large-scale visuals, and a discrete use of a template design. If you employ these techniques in your own presentations, the outcome should be equally effective.

Part Five

FORMULATING THE BRIEF THAT DRIVES GREAT CREATIVE

22

Take the Word *Brief* Seriously

I once worked at an agency where we wrote briefs that were as fat as the Manhattan Yellow Pages (well, maybe not quite that big, but you get the picture). The account guys wrote them (there were no Planners at this shop). We were so proud of these briefs. They were so thorough, so exhaustive in their detail, so exhausting to read.

The agency hired a new Creative Director, who tried working with these briefs for a few months. One day, he appeared in the doorway of my office, my latest masterwork in hand (actually in two hands; it was a two-fisted document). His expression was a combination of exasperation and despair. "This isn't a brief; it's the anti-brief!" he exclaimed.

He sat down and dropped the offending document on my desk. It landed with a solid thud. "Here's what we need," he said, as he pulled out a pen and scribbled this outline:

1. Key fact
2. Problem
3. Objective
4. Key benefit
5. Support
6. Tone
7. Audience
8. Competition
9. Mandatories

"That's it," he said. "Forget about telling me everything you know; just tell me what I *need* to know to make good advertising." Before he stomped out, he added, "And stop writing these things on your own. Get the creatives in the room with you and figure it out together."

Now, this Creative Director could have gone to any number of account people at the agency, but he came to me. I didn't know whether to be flattered or insulted, but I guess he chose me because I wrote the longest briefs of all. I'd also like to think it was because he saw there was hope for me.

I resisted at first, but ultimately did what he asked. To my astonishment, he was right. Our briefs became sharper, tighter, and more focused. The whole creative process became sharper, tighter, and more focused. The creative work that came out of those briefs was sharper, tighter, and more focused. Better still, instead of confining the work, the tighter briefs had the opposite impact. They had a liberating effect on our writers and art directors, who now felt free to explore widely in and around the direction provided in the brief.

Initially, it was a struggle to get creative people to attend sessions where we would work on the brief together. But ultimately, the whole agency adopted the new format for the brief, and the collaborative process for writing it, as the basis for creating work. In fact, the creative staff became so committed to the process that they would refuse to work on an assignment unless there was at least one session in which they participated in the development of the brief.

The version of the brief we actually adopted was not as clipped as the one the creative director wrote out in my office, but it remained very tight.

Using a form like the one below, we created briefs that were always just one or two pages. It led to some consistently excellent advertising.

There are probably as many different kinds of briefs as there are agencies. And with the emergence and growing influence of Account Planning, the development of creative briefs has taken on new dimensions since the days my agency first deployed the following form. I'm not suggesting this is the definitive brief format and that you should promptly abandon whatever your agency is currently using. What I am suggesting is that you take the word *brief* seriously. There is a saying: "I didn't have time to write you a short letter, so I wrote you a long one." That says it all.

CREATIVE STRATEGY

Account Name
Specific Assignment Name
Job Number
Date

Key Fact
A one- or two-sentence distillation of the current consumer marketing situation or environment.

(continued)

(*continued*)

What consumer problem must the advertising solve?
A precise definition, written from the consumer perspective, *not* the client perspective.

What is the objective of the advertising?
This flows from the definition of the consumer problem.

What is the most important benefit, promise, or offer?
Must be strong enough to overcome the problem and meet the objective.

What facts support this benefit, promise, or offer?
Should be a simple listing. If additional information is needed, provide an attachment.

With whom are we talking?
Provide psychographics, in addition to demographics, to the extent they are known or can be intuited.

With whom or what are we competing?
Products and services, as well as companies and internal competitors.

What should the tone of the advertising be?
Describe with a series of adjectives. Be specific, concrete, and evocative.

Are there any mandatories we must account for in the advertising?
Is there anything we must deal with, officially (such as logo size or placement) or unofficially (such as client preferences)?

Approvals:

Account _____

Creative _____

Client _____

Brevity is hard work. The key to achieving it lies not in the initial writing, but in rewriting, rewriting, and rewriting, to distill the brief to its essence. There should be no wasted words.

Brevity is crucial because a brief that isn't brief is no help to anyone. The reader can't distinguish the important points from the underbrush of detail in which they are hidden. The client won't embrace it, the creative team won't follow it, and the work will suffer because of it.

A good brief is critical to achieving great creative work. And a good brief *is* brief.

23

What Makes
a Brilliant Brief?

If you're a copywriter, you are likely known for the television, radio, print, digital, and other content you create. You are a writer of commercials.

If you're an account person, you are known for the conference reports, presentations, and scopes of work you create. You are *not* a writer of commercials; you *are* a commercial writer, with these items the product of your commerce. And as a commercial writer, one of the products of your commerce is the formulation of creative briefs.

Now, lots of agencies have Planning people who lay claim to the creative brief, and this is fair, but this does not relieve you of responsibility. You still need to assert your role as a full and contributing partner to its formulation.

If you work in an agency without a Planning department, chances are creating creative briefs lives in your domain, and presents one of the invigorating challenges of your career. If the brief is right, the advertising likely will be right. If the brief is wrong, chances are the advertising will be wrong.

As I wrote earlier, there are as many approaches to creative briefs as there are agencies, but even so, there are four things that should guide you in your efforts:

1. **It needs to be short**. Reread Chapter 22 and follow its advice. To recap: a brief that goes on for page after page is nearly useless. Your job is to sort through what's helpful and what's not, keeping the former, discarding the latter. The result is a brief that should be at most two pages, with every word carrying weight.

2. **It needs to be right**. The key to writing a brief is not the *first* draft; it's the *last* draft, with as many drafts as necessary in between to ensure the outcome is exactly right. By "right," I mean it must precisely define the audience—their needs, concerns, and aspirations—and the challenge or issue you want the advertising to address.

3. **It needs to be collaborative**. I'll talk more about this in a moment, but an inescapable reality of the advertising business are the times when, of necessity, you will write a draft on your own, then share it with others for input and commentary. But the real secret of creating a brief that works is to get in a room and draft it *together*.

   The sheer act of having multiple minds attack a challenge is the best way to solve it. It is discourse—an exchange of views—that has the best opportunity to capture moments of true insight. It is harder (maybe impossible) to do this on your own. It is far easier to do this with a small group—no more than four or five people—committed to solving the problem.

4. **It needs to be tight, so the creative people can be loose**. A tightly worded, well-crafted, and well-thought-out brief is not *limiting* to the creative people who rely on it. Instead, it is *liberating*, giving license to writers and art directors to roam freely within the borders of the brief.

There's a creative brief template you can follow on pages 121–122, but the best way to explain a brief is to show lots of examples of how different agencies approached the challenge of writing a perfectly articulated brief. I wish I could do this, but that would transform this into a book about briefs, and not a book about client service.

I can, however, share an example with you. For an insurance industry client, my colleagues at Womenkind developed the brief that follows for a series of television spots. Here is what they wrote.

CREATIVE BRIEF

What's the assignment?
Develop a DRTV campaign that will generate telephone calls to the Sales and Solution Center from qualified prospects who are: 1) interested in and ready to buy term life insurance; or 2) ready to speak to agents outside the Solutions and Sales Center, given the amount of insurance they require exceeds the company's $100K policy threshold.

What is the business problem?
The company is successful, with almost 100 percent aided awareness. However, their "house file" customer base is aging and direct mail is a category in decline.

What will solve this?
Create a DTC TV advertising campaign that introduces Term Life Direct (TLD)—a new product for younger consumers—and make consumers reconsider the importance of life insurance, and the relevance of the company.

Whom are we talking to?
There are three core audiences to consider:

1. **Dual income parents.** They are mid-30s college graduate professional women who are married with a HHI of $75K+, with young children. They are time-starved and busy. They have not saved enough for college or for retirement because

(continued)

(continued)

these things seem so far away. They put their kids' needs before their own in all other aspects of their lives.

2. **Independent single parents.** Early 40s, they are typically single moms who are working and somewhat educated. They may be divorced or just single parents but they are female heads of household who are the cornerstone of their families. They live paycheck to paycheck and are careful about money. They need simplicity in their lives and tend to live in the moment because they worry a lot about the future.

3. **Almost empty nester couples.** In their early 50s, they married young and started a family immediately, so their kids are going off to the military or college or have left home already. They struggled in the early years but life is becoming a little easier. They have equity in their homes but have not saved enough for retirement. Aware of their mortality for the first time, they may be starting to suffer from ailments and worry a little about their health in the future.

What do they think of us?

They have heard of the company, and may have some recall of the brand advertising. But they don't perceive the firm as different or better. Many believe that life insurance is just one of those things that they should have but that they haven't gotten round to—like making a will or saving more for college or retirement. The money is for a "just in case" scenario and they have bills to pay now and investments to make for the future—life insurance is a dead end, because they will never get to see a return on the investment anyway.

What do we want them to think?

A life insurance policy is not a dead-end expense. It's an *investment in your family's future*—just like investing in college fees or retirement funds. A TLD policy will give you peace of mind because it helps you invest in the future of those you love in the event that you are no longer there to support them. You put your family before yourself in everything else you do—so keep doing it—get a TLD policy from the company.

What is the single thought that will get them there?
TLD is a simple, affordable way for you to invest in your family's future—even if you are no longer around.

Why should they believe this?
- Get $100K coverage for as little as $23.20 a month
- Get a quote in five minutes, coverage in three days
- If you lose your job, we'll pay your premium for up to six months
- No medical exam necessary
- 90 percent of claims are paid within one week

Tone & manner
Level-headed, upbeat, credible, candid, trustworthy
   Advertising must be consistent with and complementary to the client's brand advertising campaign.

Media requirements
Three: 60s, to air September 15.

Legal requirements
To come. There will be boilerplate legal language, provided by the company, which will need to appear on screen.

Executional mandatories
- Use the company tagline

   Key dates:

Present creative:	W/O May 5
Filing:	May 19–June 9
Award job to director:	W/O July 14
Prep:	July 14–July 28
Shoot:	W/O August 4
Post-production:	August 11–25
Ship:	W/O September 1
On air:	Monday, September 15

Okay, I did say two pages max, and this runs a little longer than this. And I did say, "Perfectly articulated," and this is far from that. But this brief shows you how Womenkind organized information into key categories, and the way in which they addressed those categories.

The section I'd like you to take a closer look at is "Who are we talking to," which discusses the advertising's target audience. Most creative briefs confine the description to the facts, things like age, income, and marital status. The brief you see here goes beyond that, with a description that begins to explore attitude, belief, and circumstances. This is a substantial improvement but even it falls short.

What's needed is a fuller exploration of, dare I say it, the character of not the audience, but of the individual person who is within that audience. What does he or she think, feel, and believe? What prevents him from acting? What motivates her to respond? Are there different characters in the audience, each bringing their own point of view to the proceedings?

These are things you normally cannot get at through data. Chapter 25 of this book is called, "Know When to Look It Up; Know When to Make It Up." This is one of those "make it up" moments. And what we are going to make up is a *persona*, an imagined, highly creative narrative, written in a third-person voice that expresses the thoughts, feelings, and beliefs previously unavailable to us.

This is what Womenkind did to supplement the creative brief for that insurance company. They, in fact, wrote three personas, each reflecting a different segment of the market. Here's what Womenkind wrote for one of the three segments, for someone they referred to as "Rhonda":

Rhonda is 42. She's a single mother. She has one child. She works as an admin in a construction company. She went to college, but didn't finish.

Her divorce eight years ago threw her for a loop. She's fully aware of how quickly life can change, circumstances can change, and she's become a very cautious person as a result.

As a single mom, head of household, be-all and end-all, she feels like everything falls on her. She's the cornerstone of her family, and she never lets herself lose sight of that responsibility.

She worries about the future as a matter of course. But she's got lots of worries and she's constantly reordering her priorities.

Rhonda is careful about money. She knows the price of everything she puts into her cart at the grocery store and doesn't mind putting items back she doesn't need. It's her own form of financial security.

She's a strong woman who's easily intimidated by formality. She avoids complications in life and always seeks the simple, direct solution.

This image of Rhonda helped the creative team gain a fuller, deeper understanding of one segment of their target, helping them create advertising with an authentic voice that connected with consumers.

Speaking of "voice," I cannot overemphasize how critical this is to the creative process. The creative brief includes a section called, "Tone & manner," and this helps guide the creative team, but capturing the essence of voice extends well beyond that, and is utterly key to crafting creative that's meaningful, motivating, and differentiating.

As I think about creative briefs and how to do them well, I am reminded that Ammirati & Puris co-founder Martin Puris used to say that 80 percent of all creative work fails before one word of copy is written. That's because if the strategy is wrong, there is little hope of getting the advertising right.

So how do you get the strategy right? Certainly not by sitting in your office alone, banging out the strategy brief in isolation. Even if your agency has an Account Planning department, and the Planners are responsible for leading creative strategy development, you don't want them writing the brief on their own.

You get the strategy right by recognizing that developing the strategy is a team sport, and the creative crew—the writer and art director assigned to work on the ad or the campaign—are critical team members. You shouldn't just hand them a brief; you should work with them to create the brief.

There are three reasons to do this.

1. It helps the creative team become immersed in the assignment and take ownership of it. The creative team's active participation ensures that the brief that emerges from the development process actually will assist in the creation of effective advertising.

2. The creative team will unearth issues or gaps in knowledge, which gives you an early opportunity to address them.

3. The creative team will uncover insights or help make connections that otherwise might be missed. Writers and art directors generally see things from a perspective different from yours. You want to capture that perspective early on in the creative process, during the development of the brief that will drive the work.

Thinking about what Martin Puris said, I'm reminded that there's one other reason to involve the creative team: to ensure that the advertising that results is among the 20 percent that succeeds, not the 80 percent that fails.

24

In Writing the Brief, Provide the Client's Perspective

One of your key roles is to represent the client within the agency to your colleagues. In fact, no one in your agency should know the client better than you do. You want to be the first person that agency staffers turn to when they want to know something about your client. That means making yourself an expert on your client's products, people, and culture. Here's how to do that.

- *Spend as much time in your client's offices as you do your own.* It's amazing how much you can learn by walking the halls, eating in the cafeteria, and generally seeing first-hand how the company works.

- *Get out in the field.* Nothing is more valuable than meeting your client's customers and hearing their issues and concerns. Traveling with the salespeople who serve those customers gives you an opportunity to get their front-line perspective on the company, its customers, and its competitors.

- *Spend time with your clients away from the office.* If I have a meeting scheduled with an out-of-town client, I make it a point to arrive the evening before. I schedule a dinner for that evening with one of my key client contacts. I schedule a breakfast the following morning with a different client contact. I'll have lunch that day with yet a third client contact.

  My purpose isn't to run up a big entertainment bill. My purpose is to use that time away from the client's office not only to talk business, but also to really get to know my clients, to understand their professional and personal goals. I also use that time to uncover any issues and concerns with the agency and its work that might not be readily visible. It's not that I learn *more* things in these out-of-the-office sessions with clients; I learn *different* things.

- *Read the trades.* Virtually every industry has publications that cover the field. You should become a subscriber and a regular reader. While we're on the subject of reading, you should not only read your client's annual report, you should regularly visit the company's website to check for the latest product announcements, news releases, white papers, speeches, and other materials.

- *Watch the competition.* You should gather everything you can on the competition: advertising, articles, speeches by management, Wall Street analyst reports, social media commentary, and anything else that's available. At least twice a year, you should provide a synthesis and an analysis of the competitive landscape, for the benefit of both your client and your colleagues on the account.

- *Be a customer.* You should buy the products and services your client sells. The purchasing process can be telling. By using the product or service, by being a customer, you can better understand what other customers experience.

Doing these things gives you a perspective that can help sharpen and define the marketing and creative strategy the agency develops to drive creative work. It also can help uncover the overlooked fact that may drive an insight that results in killer advertising.

Here's an example of what I mean. Back in the 1980s, Ammirati & Puris created a wonderful advertising campaign for UPS. The tagline for the campaign was, "We run the tightest ship in the shipping business." One of the commercials in that award-winning campaign was called "Washing Planes." It explained that the frequent washing of planes helped reduce air drag, which in turn reduced fuel consumption, which in turn helped UPS be more efficient and thus allowed the company to charge lower prices for overnight delivery than Federal Express.

How did the agency discover that washing planes makes them more efficient in the air? It's not as if someone at UPS said, "Hey let's make a commercial about how clean we keep our planes." Instead, it came from the agency team immersing itself in the UPS culture. That little-known fact became the basis of a smart, engaging, and memorable commercial that had a big impact.

Once you have a finished brief ready to share with your client, there remains one last obstacle to overcome: I call it *brief amnesia*, an illness that often defies diagnosis. You might think it's about a short-term memory loss—hence the phrase—but it's not. Instead, it's a form of amnesia that is about getting your clients to actually approve the brief.

Here's how the illness strikes.

You send a creative brief to your client for review and approval. The client, up to her eyeballs in work, gives the brief the once-over. When you follow up with a call to see if the client has changes or input, the client says, "Looks good to me; let's go with it."

The creative team develops ad concepts based on the brief. You and the creative team present them to the client. The client rejects the work. You ask why. The client gives a reason that has nothing to do with the creative brief. You respond that the work is on strategy. The client barely remembers the strategy, let alone that she approved it. If she does remember, she doesn't care.

Instead, she uses the concepts in front of her to re-engineer the strategy. You and your colleagues return to the agency. You start over from the beginning, developing a new brief.

That's brief amnesia at work.

So how do you immunize your client against this dreadful disease? There's only one way: make the client part of the process of developing the creative brief.

Here's what to do: ask the client to do a full-scale download at the start of the assignment. Ideally, this takes place in a face-to-face meeting, but schedules being what they are, if you have to do it in a conference call, so be it.

What you're looking for from your client is (1) a clear statement of what the client wants to accomplish with the advertising; (2) all the facts related to the product or service that is the subject of the advertising, including the audience to which it is to be directed; and (3) any mandatories the agency must take into account in developing the advertising.

Armed with this information, supplemented with background materials you gather independently, develop the brief. Once you and the team are satisfied with it, don't send it to the client. Take it to the client, and take the client through it. Extract additional input. Be alert to any concerns that arise. Go back and revise the brief if necessary, but make sure that the client is completely clear and completely comfortable with it.

Then make the client sign it.

It's amazing how this simple act will make a client take notice. It says, "I'm taking ownership of this. I approve it, and I understand that my advertising will be based on it."

That's how you cure brief amnesia.

This is critical not only because the brief will guide creative development, but also because the brief serves as a yardstick by which to measure the concepts that emerge from it. You and your colleagues will use the brief to evaluate creative concepts before you show them to the client. You will make sure that each concept reflects the brief and is on strategy.

Then, when you present creative work to the client, it's a whole lot less likely that she'll use the work to reinvent the strategy.

What if there's a really great concept the creative team comes up with, but it's not on strategy? You explain to the client, "During creative development, we came up with another idea. We were going to discard it because it's clearly not on strategy. But we decided not to, because it's pretty compelling. We thought we'd show it to you."

Then you show it. If the client loves it, you'll have an interesting conversation and a decision to make. If the client doesn't love it, no problem. You've already presented great ideas that are on strategy.

The most important thing to remember is that to avoid brief amnesia, and to preempt clients from using the concept presentation to reinvent the strategy, make your client a partner in the development of the brief.

25

Know When to Look It Up; Know When to Make It Up

I was working with some colleagues on an advertising assignment for Myers's rum. We were struggling with the rum's dark color. "People think of rum as being clear," said one of my colleagues. "I don't know," I said, "I don't think rum is supposed to be clear. The way I see it, Myers's is the color of rum." One of my colleagues replied, "That's it! That's the line: Myers's *is* the color of rum." We used it in our advertising. Our client loved it.

Another time, this same group of colleagues and I struggled to devise a name for a customer loyalty program we were developing for Polaroid. The reward for using Polaroid cameras and film was going to be frequent flyer mileage. We didn't know what to call it. Out of the blue, one of my colleagues said, "Let's call it the *Polaroid Frequent Smileage Program.*" We loved it, the client loved it, and that's what we named the program.

I was recently sitting around at a conference room table, surrounded by a sea of paper, working with a colleague on a brand positioning assignment for a client. We were early on in the process; we hadn't even completed our research. But we were talking about finding a positioning the client could own, one that would speak to the company's strengths and would energize its employees.

We took a break. While sitting there, three words came into my head. When we reconvened, I told my colleague, "I have an idea. I don't know if it's worth a damn or not, but let me try it on you." I wrote the three words on a sheet of paper and held it up. "What do you think?" I asked. "Does it work?"

It did indeed work. It was a creative leap, right past the positioning to a tagline. All our work to date validated those three words. We would have to see if it held up. If it did, we knew what our positioning recommendation would be.

You can spend weeks, even months, immersed in research, but insights often come in a flash of recognition.

One clear insight is worth a thousand data points. You still need to do the heavy lifting in the marketplace—the customer research, the competitive analysis, the field visits—but there comes a time when you should put the research away and go with your instinct. Sometimes too much data can interfere with understanding. The secret is to combine what you know with what you feel in order to push for new ideas and better solutions.

If you can do that, you have a future in this business.

Part Six

ESTABLISHING TRUST WITH CLIENTS

26

Great Work Wins Business; a Great Relationship Keeps It

In new business pitches, clients often claim to seek a relationship with an agency, yet select the winner based on which shop presented the work they liked best. Conversely, with existing accounts, clients often say it's the work that matters, yet fire their agency because of a breakdown in the relationship.

Think of all the client-agency marriages that dissolved, even though they were characterized by great work. BMW and Ammirati & Puris. Ikea and Deutsch. Taco Bell and TBWA\Chiat\Day. Charles Schwab and BBDO. Staples and Cliff Freeman. Add your own examples. The list can get very, very long.

I remember what one client said to me years ago: "I love your work; the agency is very creative. But you guys are just too hard to deal with; everything is a fight. If I have to choose, I'll take an agency a little less talented but a whole lot easier to work with."

And then she fired us.

We had won the account based on our work. We lost the account because we didn't understand that while great work is what wins business, a great relationship is what keeps it. We thought if we did great work, the relationship stuff would take care of itself. Advertising isn't just a creative business, though; it's a relationship business.

I don't mean relationship as in "doing lunch," although there certainly is a time and place for that. I mean relationship as in doing all of the things, and being all of the things, that build trust with the client. Listening. Asking the right questions. Anticipating and solving problems. Meeting commitments. Managing expectations. Eliminating unpleasant surprises. Taking ownership. Acting with integrity.

A client who trusts you will seek your counsel. A client who trusts you will forgive your honest mistakes, and will work with you to correct them. A client who trusts you will partner with you in taking the risks that lead to great work.

A relationship is like a brand: you have to invest in it, and understand that it gets built over time. You can't rush it; even the slightest hint of insincerity, dishonesty, or manipulation will kill a relationship before it has a chance to develop.

Whenever I hear someone say, "The work is the only thing that matters," I think of the client who fired me years ago. It reminds me that if you don't pay attention to building a strong relationship with your client, you run the risk of being shown the door, no matter how terrific the work.

Advertising *is* about the work, but remember that advertising is a business. Business is about relationships, and a great relationship allows great work to flourish.

27

Client Presentations Are as Important as New Business Presentations

Agencies treat new business presentations with the intensity and urgency of opening night at the theater.

Everyone knows what's at stake. There is careful consideration given to casting the presenters. There is heavy investment in staging and props. Every word of the script is thought through. The pitch team rehearses. Then it rehearses some more.

But with existing clients, everyone at the agency is so busy making the work that they often neglect the presenting part. With clients demanding faster and faster turnaround, and with agency staffs sliced to the bone because of financial pressures, the problem has grown acute. Almost every account person I know can tell stories of flying out the door to make a client meeting while jamming work completed just minutes ago onto a laptop, thumb drive, or presentation case. Rehearsal, such as it is, takes place in the 15-minute cab ride to the client's office.

Yet client presentations are at least as important as new business presentations, if not more so. The stakes are just as high, if not higher. The only thing worse than losing a new business pitch is losing a client. If you don't pay attention to client presentations, if you take them for granted, that is the risk.

Client presentations, like new business presentations, are about theater. A bad presentation, like bad theater, often leads to a bad ending, with the client unhappy and the agency scrambling to regroup. A good presentation usually leads to a happy ending, with the client satisfied and the work approved.

A good presentation is no accident. It requires proper casting, with an eye to who can best deliver the material. It requires thoughtful preparation, with particular attention paid to anticipating client concerns and how best to address them. Above all, it requires sufficient time to rehearse, to ensure everyone understands his or her role and how to play it. Many of the recommendations I included about new business in Chapter 6, *How to Contribute Before, During, and After Pitch Day*, apply here. It you need a refresher, I suggest you read that chapter again.

Agencies that understand the importance of rehearsing for new business presentations often forget that rehearsing for client presentations is equally important.

Part of the problem is that many agency people hate rehearsing and will do everything to avoid it, no matter how much time there is in the schedule. They find rehearsing awkward, embarrassing, or even a little intimidating. They have a point. It can be harder to stand up in front of colleagues than in front of clients. But doing so can make a huge difference in your team's presentation and professionalism.

Rehearsal helps you discover holes in your argument. It helps you anticipate the questions and concerns the client might raise. It polishes your delivery. It allows you to work out the hand-offs among the team members. It gives everyone in the group an opportunity to help strengthen each member's part. It can build your confidence. For all these reasons, you should remind your colleagues that, no matter how pressed for time all of you are, no matter how tight the schedule, having a rehearsal might make the difference between success and failure. Then you should take ownership of the rehearsal process.

Set the rehearsal time, drag people into the conference room, get them to agree on their roles, get everyone to agree on the agency recommendation (if what you're presenting is creative work), and then make them stand up and present their parts. The more time you spend, the better you will be. Even if the run-through is lightning fast, it's better than no rehearsal time.

Still, I'm a realist. I know there will be times when a rehearsal just won't happen. You and your colleagues will race out of the agency to get to the client on time, then wing it once you're there. What follows is a perfect example of what can, and often does, go wrong, when you don't make time for rehearsal.

My agency team and I were presenting a new campaign to the client. One of the team members, a young copywriter, was standing at the head of a long conference table, in front of a sea of expectant faces, including our main client's boss, the company's senior vice president of marketing. It was a big day, a big room, and a big group of clients.

The presentation started well enough. I had done the setup for the writer, taking the audience through a restatement of the assignment and a quick recap of the creative brief. I turned to the copywriter. "Let me turn this over to Jane, our Associate Creative Director."

Jane rose from her chair. You immediately could sense something was wrong. That "something" was fear. Jane was terrified. It quickly became apparent that everything she wanted to say had fled from her head. "Uh, ah, why don't I just go right to the work?" she said, and with that she pulled out the presentation boards.

We had three concepts to show. Jane raced through each one in about a minute, and couldn't wait to be done with them. Instead of relishing the moment and being equal to it, she was overwhelmed by it. I wanted to rescue her, but any intervention on my part would only have added to her humiliation.

Our clients were sympathetic, their response muted, their questions restrained. But they didn't buy a single idea we presented. We promised to come back in three days with new work.

After the meeting ended, my primary client contact took me aside. "What happened up there?" she asked, pointing to the front of the room. "I really don't know," I responded, "I'm sorry. I thought we were prepared. It's clear we weren't." I assured my client that for the next presentation, the creative director would be there and would take the lead. The client's only response was, "I'd better go see my boss. I might as well take my beating now."

We embarrassed ourselves. We embarrassed our client in front of her boss. We undermined our grip on the account. But the biggest damage was to Jane, who was shaken by her meltdown. "I don't know what happened to me," she said. "I just lost it. It's never happened before."

It wasn't the writer's fault. It was mine. Jane clearly was over-matched by the challenge of making a big presentation to an important client in an intimidating environment. I should have insisted her boss make the presentation. I had thought this would be a good opportunity, an occasion she would rise to. I was so wrong. It's a lesson I've never forgotten.

It's important to give more junior people a chance to present. How else will they learn? But those learning opportunities need to be confined to *internal* agency presentations—the young copywriter to the creative director, the young account executive to the group account director—until that star of the future has earned a role in the present, and is proven ready to perform in front of the client.

Until that time, presenting to the client should be left to those most effective at it, and that usually means the more senior people in the shop (any senior person who is a weak presenter needs to address that weakness). There is too much riding on the presentation to do otherwise.

You are not only presenting work, you are representing the agency. Every presentation offers an opportunity to validate the client's confidence in the agency, or conversely, to undermine it.

There should be no understudies on presentation day. That's when the veterans, the stars, should perform. That's what the client has a right to expect. That is what the client is paying for. That is what will keep the business right where it is, at your agency.

28

Always Ask, "Does This Advertising Pass the 'So What' Test?"

The airwaves are filled with ads that, at best, put the viewer to sleep. At worst, they debase the client's brand, rather than build it.

It is not enough for the work to be on strategy. It has to engage consumers and make them want to pay attention. You can't influence how people think and act with boring advertising. To achieve those results requires advertising driven by a smart, honest, and emotionally true idea.

Whenever you're reviewing work with your creative colleagues, first ask yourself if it is on strategy. Then ask yourself if it makes you think, "So what?" As in, "so what's this advertising about, and why should I care? Actually I don't care at all for this work."

Advertising like this is dead from the outset, and is easily dismissed or ignored, or worse, disliked. It doesn't attract or hold attention, let alone motivate people to act.

If the work doesn't pass this test, it will not pass the test of the marketplace. This isn't work that should go to the client. It is better, instead, to keep working, and to keep pushing for a solution that passes the "So what" test.

29

Don't Fall in Love with Good Work; Don't Fall for Bad Work

There were safer alternatives on the wall, but my creative colleagues and I were convinced that one particular concept was right for the client. We were, however, having trouble convincing our boss, the head of the agency. We must have argued for an hour. He wanted to kill the idea. We wanted to make it our recommendation.

We took a break. The boss and I had a little conversation on our own.

"We can't go with that campaign as the recommendation," he said. "It's too risky and the client will never buy it."

"It is risky," I conceded, "but not because it's wrong, or because it's off strategy. It's risky because the client has never seen anything like this from us before, and it's not what she's expecting. We'd be crazy to kill it without at least showing it to her. It's just too good."

"I really don't like it," my boss persisted.

"But all of us do," I countered. "If it were off strategy, I'd agree with you, but it isn't. It delivers perfectly on the strategy. It's brilliant and funny. There's a real idea at work. And it will have legs."

"I still don't like it." I could hear the frustration in his voice, but I wasn't going to give in.

"Look, do you really want to overrule me, the creative director, the writer, and the art director? It's four against one."

"Since when are all votes created equal?" he replied testily.

"Since never," I conceded. "But you yourself said it's my account to run. I'm asking you to trust my judgment. I know this client better than you do. They will love this work, and they're going to buy it."

"That's what I'm afraid of!" my boss exclaimed.

In the end, he backed off, grudgingly, reluctantly, fearfully. We could present the idea we were so in love with, but we also agreed to present four concepts instead of three, so the client would still have three ideas to choose from that my boss felt comfortable with.

Why did we fight so hard for this one particular idea? We had three other perfectly good concepts to go with—and that was the problem.

Good work is on strategy. It's smart, respects the viewer, and is well crafted. You can produce it on time and on budget. Your client can greenlight it. It makes you comfortable.

Good work is the enemy of great work. If you are satisfied with work that is merely good, you will never deliver great work for your clients.

Great work, like good work, is on strategy. But it's beyond smart; it's something else. Something rare and special. It doesn't just respect the viewer, it connects with the viewer.

Great work might make you uncomfortable. It might be something startlingly new. It might take risks. You might not be able to produce it on time or within budget, and your client might not readily say yes to it.

If the work is truly great, and right for your client, your job is to support it and to help your client see its potential and choose to buy it.

The idea my colleagues and I were fighting for was great, not merely good. It was visually stunning. It spoke the language of the target audience. More than anything else, it was hilariously funny, and humor was the right way to go in this instance.

You might be wondering what happened in the client presentation. The client laughed when we showed the idea to her. She got it, she knew the target would get it. In the end, she didn't love it enough to take a risk on it. The very thing that made the work great—the humor—was the thing that worried her. So she went with a safer choice.

The fault was ours, not hers. We knew the idea was right. We did our best to be persuasive, without applying undue pressure. We wanted her to own the idea with us. We didn't succeed.

We wound up executing a different concept, which made perfectly good advertising. We liked it, and so did the client. But it wasn't great, and we didn't love it.

That was a missed opportunity. But what happens when you're looking at work that is little more than a clever execution or an unusual production technique?

Work like this can be insidious. It masquerades as great advertising, but it is not. It instead sacrifices the client's advertising objective on an altar of creative self-indulgence. Okay, I admit the metaphor is a little overwrought, but you get the picture.

This kind of advertising is bad, and to see it for what it is requires judgment, dispassion, and discipline.

It's a much happier task to stand up for work you believe in than it is to speak out against work you know is wrong. But your colleagues will listen to you if you've established yourself as a credible source of input, if you speak with conviction, and if your assessment is well-reasoned.

It's not enough to simply say, "I don't know why, but I just don't like it," or "The client won't buy it." You need to explain why the work doesn't deliver on the strategy, why it will fail to engage viewers, why it doesn't deliver the message clearly, or whatever else might be wrong with it.

The easiest way to spot work like this is to ask, "What's the idea driving this advertising?" If there's no idea in what you're seeing, then there isn't anything for the client to buy, and the agency shouldn't be trying to sell it.

30

Choice Is Good

I've heard of agencies that present just one creative concept to their clients. I've never worked at such an agency, so I can only guess at the motivation behind this approach. Perhaps it's to show confidence that the agency has arrived at *the* solution. Perhaps it's that the agency doesn't have any other ideas.

The agencies I worked at, and most of the other agencies I'm familiar with, have lots of ideas. They know there's more than one way to execute a strategy.

Always bring your client more than one concept. What's the right number? It depends on the client.

Some clients love to see the conference room walls papered with a dozen or more ideas. But that takes time and costs money. It's not always possible, practical, or even desirable. With many clients, showing more than five concepts can be confusing. It also can imply you are surrounding the strategic challenge, rather than solving it.

Generally, the right number of concepts to present is three. It's large enough to provide the client meaningful choice, yet small enough to compel the agency to select only the very best ideas to present.

What do you do if your creative team comes up with only one or two ideas? Do you go to the client with just that one or two? With rare exceptions, I would say no. The best creative people usually have lots of ideas to show you, and if one thing isn't working, they always have something else, or are comfortable going back and concepting some additional ideas. Less talented creative people often have just a single idea to offer, so they will fight fiercely for that idea, regardless of its merit, because they are not confident they can produce more.

It's a matter of knowing your creative team. If you know it will fall short in generating ideas, you need to encourage the creative director to add a second or even a third team to the creative development process. This is not an easy conversation to have, but it's better to deal with this issue at the agency, well before the client presentation, than to go to the client with only the thinnest of presentations. If you do that, you usually wind up going back to the agency anyway to develop more ideas, which costs you time and client goodwill.

Here are three other things to keep in mind when deciding which work to present to the client:

1. Before you present, agree among yourselves what the agency recommendation is, why it is the recommendation, and why the others are not.

2. Decide who will speak for the agency on the recommendation.

3. Make sure you would be proud to execute any of the concepts you show. Eliminate any straw men before the presentation. If it isn't good enough to execute, it isn't good enough to present.

31

Fight About the Work with Colleagues; Fight for It with Clients

Years ago, when I was running a major financial services account, I worked with one of my creative director colleagues on a print ad campaign. I'll call him Myron. Myron was a very senior, veteran guy. It was a day or two before we were scheduled to present to the client, and he was walking me through the concepts he was going to show.

Myron was the type of writer who liked to crowd the walls with ideas. It was typical of him to show a dozen or more approaches. For some clients, that many choices would be paralyzing. Not this client. This client loved the theater of it. He loved to debate the ads. He really took ownership of the work, and that was great for us. He welcomed a room full of ideas.

So there I was, looking with Myron at maybe 15 ideas slapped up on the walls of the agency conference room. I liked maybe five of them. Another five or six were serviceable. The rest, I thought, were losers.

Overall, I felt great about what I was looking at and said so. I made some suggestions on a couple of the executions. Then I said, "There are a few ads that aren't working." I explained why. In two instances, Myron agreed, and decided to kill the ideas. We disagreed about two or three others. I made my case: the weaker executions would dilute the whole presentation. Besides, we didn't need that many options.

The problem was, Myron thought a couple of the ads I didn't like were among the strongest on the wall. So we went back and forth for a while. Our disagreement never reached cage-match intensity, but let's just say it got pretty spirited. Myron put an end to the debate by saying he'd think about it. That's all I could ask for. If I couldn't persuade him, then the problem was mine, not his.

Two days later we met with the client. Myron took the client through the work. The client liked much of it, but there were two ideas he gravitated to. One was a favorite of mine, the other was one of the ads I wanted to kill, but Myron kept it.

The client turned to me and asked, "So which one would you go with?"

It would have been easy for me to support my choice and trash the one I didn't like. Easy, but wrong.

You owe your colleagues an insightful, expert, candid, and sensitive assessment of their work. (By *work*, I don't just mean creative; it could be a strategy recommendation, or a media plan, or something else.) You should base this assessment on your knowledge of the market, your grasp of the consumer's needs and interests, and your understanding of client expectations and culture.

You and your colleagues won't always agree. You will argue. This often is part of arriving at the right solution.

It's fine to fight about the work in private, but once you've agreed on what to present to the client, get on the bus. When you are in front of the client, never throw the work, or your colleagues, under the bus.

I didn't throw the ad I didn't like under the bus. I supported it, and I also supported my choice. But the client wanted a definitive recommendation. Of course, Myron and I were prepared to make one. We agreed before the meeting which one we would go with. So I turned to Myron and said, "Why don't you talk about the choice we arrived at."

Myron did. You probably want to know which one we recommended. The funny thing is, I can't remember. What I do remember is that I fought about the work with my colleague, but fought for it with my client.

32

Do Not Sell

W. David Vining, the former director of U.S. advertising and direct marketing at Compaq Computer (now HP) and now Vice President of Corporate Partnerships at CoreNet Global, once said, "Too often, a creative-driven agency will try to force their own ideas on a client, rather than working in a spirit of collaboration. It takes a very strong account person to maintain the client's interest, and not take the easy way out by simply selling the work."

David is certainly not alone in this view. I know other clients who share a similar belief.

The problem with selling is that it's about applying pressure on a buyer to do what you want—what is best for you, your colleagues, your agency. Account people often are tempted to be salespeople. By selling the client on the agency's recommendation, you might prove your worth to your colleagues, especially the creative folks. But you will pay a dear price if you take this approach.

You want your client to buy great work. Great work almost always entails an element of risk because there is inevitably something new or unexpected about it. Clients generally will take risks with people they trust. An account person who is busy selling a client is not likely to build trust with that client.

Conversely, an account person who understands that the client's interests are the agency's top priority is going to be viewed as a trusted partner, not as a salesperson for the agency's interests. That kind of account person is in a much better position to credibly recommend that the client take the risk on great work. In the end, that account person is the creative team's greatest ally.

I should be clear about one thing: when I say an account person should make the client's interests the agency's top priority, I am *not* suggesting that the account person is there to simply do the client's bidding or to merely follow the client's commands. Quite the opposite is true. The account person who has established credibility with a client is in the best position to challenge, when necessary, that client's assumptions, demands, and opinions.

Great account people do not sell. Instead, they serve as partners to both their colleagues and to their clients, with a responsibility to facilitate the creation of great work, and a goal of helping clients make the right decisions about that work.

33

Bring Your Clients into the Process Early and Often

Most of my clients have forgotten more than I ever knew about their companies and their brands, and that's not because I wasn't immersed in their business. It's just that my clients bring years of experience to the table, experience working inside their companies, experience I could never begin to fully comprehend, let alone duplicate.

I've always understood the benefit of taking advantage of that. At the onset of a new relationship or a new assignment, I tell my clients, "The agency is going to work incredibly hard on this, but we're going to ask you to work hard with us. We need you to be actively involved. We can't do great work for you unless you help us."

Then I ask the clients to outline what they expect from the agency and how they would like to work.

Having this kind of client input helps avoid false starts. Early involvement also gives the client a sense of ownership of the work. This is incredibly important when it comes time for the client to champion the work to the company's employees and management.

So don't hesitate to get your client involved early and often. The work will be better for it, as will the process of creating it.

34

Respect What It Takes to Do Great Creative

My colleagues and I used to love to present to one particular client.

He was a very senior, very veteran, very smart guy. Whenever we would present, he would listen with great concentration. He would rarely interrupt. He would instead let us go through all the concepts and options we had prepared for his review.

When we were done, he would stand up to address us. We presented to him many times, but his initial response would always go something like this: "First, I want to thank all of you for your hard work. It's clear from the presentation that you put a tremendous amount of thought and effort into the assignment, and I appreciate that. And there are some terrific ads on the table. Now let's go through each of the concepts one by one so I can give you feedback."

Sometimes the input was minor. Most of the time it was significant and as a result we had to re-concept. No one ever complained. Creative people loved this client and would do anything for him. We did work for him that was the best the agency could do.

What was this client's secret? It was simple. No matter what we presented, no matter how great, how good, or how average it was, this client invariably expressed respect for the work and the people who made it. That was a great lesson for me.

In my early days as an account person, I usually ran roughshod over creative people and their work. Writers and art directors would show me concepts and I'd immediately say what was wrong with them. It didn't matter that I might be right; I was serving up the input wrong, and creative people simply tuned me out.

I didn't understand that my job was to *improve* the work, not *approve* it. If I had made that one small adjustment in language and attitude, it would have made a big difference in the way I looked at creative work.

I also didn't respect what it takes to do great creative. What it takes is enormous emotional commitment. When writers or art directors show their work, they are sharing a piece of themselves. They have sweated those ideas to life, and they know they are only as good as their last idea. If you don't respect that—and in the beginning I didn't, but I learned—you have no hope of helping to make the work better.

While it takes emotional commitment to make creative work, it takes emotional detachment to make it better. Creative people don't always have the emotional detachment to evaluate and improve their work. Sometimes they mistake good work for great work. On occasion, they might even mistake bad work for great work.

Who can blame them, given what it takes to produce work in the first place? That's where smart, sensitive account people can, with great judgment and diplomacy, make a big contribution. They can provide the necessary emotional detachment to make the work better, or to prevent bad work from seeing the light of day.

You can't go about this the way I used to, by launching in with a salvo of criticism. There's a better way to provide feedback.

For example, if you're looking at a range of ideas and some are killers, some have potential, and some need to be killed, start with the killer ideas. Acknowledge them, praise them, and explain what you love about them and why.

Then with the ideas that have potential, start with what's right about each one. Praise what's working. Then talk about what's not working and why. Suggest how these ideas can be made better.

Tackle the ideas that deserve an early death last. Even here, with ideas you think are marginal at best, there is probably something you like about each of them. Find that one thing and acknowledge it before explaining why you think the ideas should be abandoned in favor of the stronger ones. If there are lots of good and even great ideas on the table, this should be relatively painless, unless you and the creative team don't agree. If that's the case, keep an open mind as to why the creative people like an idea that you don't. Perhaps you can be persuaded. Perhaps you can persuade them. You're going to need to reach an agreement, because when you visit the client, you want to present a unified front.

Keep your personal preferences out of the discussion. You are not there to render judgment on whether or not periwinkle is the right color. However, if you know the client hates periwinkle, or if periwinkle is the competitor's brand color, by all means speak up.

Here's an example of what I mean. I remember being in a pre-production meeting in which we were going over the casting for a photo shoot. We were looking at head shots of kids. Everyone liked this adorable redheaded boy. That's when I spoke up. "The client doesn't like redheaded children; they remind her of clowns and she thinks clowns are scary."

Everybody looked at me as if I were crazy. They were right; this *was* crazy.

I explained that this had come up before, on another assignment for this client, when I was working with a different creative team. "You can go in with the redheaded kid," I said, "but I'd have a backup if I were you. And don't be surprised if the client gets annoyed about your recommendation."

There were lots of cute kids to choose from. We went with another kid. It wasn't worth fighting over hair color.

In reviewing the creative work, your job is to ensure the work is on strategy, to bring a client perspective to the discussion, to measure the work against what is going on in the category, to help determine if the work passes the "So what?" test, and to ensure that no mandatory has been missed (like no redheaded kids).

Above all, your job is to push for great, if what you're seeing is merely good.

35

Credit Is for Creative Directors

Did you see the film *Wag the Dog*? The character played by Dustin Hoffman is called Stanley Motss. Stanley is a movie producer. At one point in the movie he does a riff on how everyone knows what the directors and actors do, but no one understands what a producer does. Later, he insists, "I want the credit!" Instead of getting the credit, he gets murdered. A lesson to us all.

Poor Stanley might just as well have been an agency account executive. If you're worried about getting the credit, I suggest you think about another line of work. As an account exec, your job is to give the credit—to your clients, to your colleagues—not to take it. Often, the only people who truly appreciate what you do are other account people.

Years ago, a creative team I was working with wanted to present some envelope-pushing work to our client. I knew my client tended to quickly kill new thinking if it made her even slightly nervous. So I called the client the day before the presentation and said, "Do you have time for dinner this evening?" She did.

We went without anyone else from the agency or her company. We had a great time talking about everything except work. When the time was right, I said, "Look, you're going to see some great concepts tomorrow. The creative team worked incredibly hard on the assignment, and they're really excited about what they have to show you. All of the work is really smart, but some of the best stuff is pretty edgy. Try to keep an open mind. If something concerns you, let's not kill it out of hand. Let's talk about it first."

She agreed.

The next day, the presentation went really well, and the client bought the agency's recommendation. On the way back to the agency office, the creative director said, "That was a surprise. I was expecting a fight. I wasn't expecting the client to approve our recommendation." My response was simply, "The work was great, and you did an amazing job presenting it." Then I smiled. I knew I had helped achieve the right outcome, and that was good enough for me. The creative team could have the credit. They earned it.

36

We Are Smarter Together Than We Are Alone

At the signing of the Declaration of Independence, Benjamin Franklin said to his Continental Congress colleagues, "We must all hang together, or assuredly, we shall all hang separately." Ben, of course, was worried about the British. The reason I pay attention to Ben is that I worry about the enemies of great advertising.

The creation of advertising and everything that surrounds it—the plans, presentations, budgets, and schedules—is a collaborative process. Effective collaboration is key to making great advertising. So why are so many agencies siloed? Why do departments within agencies—account management, creative, production—often act more like competitors than colleagues? Why is it that many agencies are characterized by turf battles, warring egos, and petty politics?

I suppose you could excuse some of this because of the inherently nonlinear, dysfunctional nature of creating advertising.

Some of this is due to the people themselves, the ones who put their interests ahead of others, often at the expense of the agency. But much of it, I think, is the result of people forgetting who and what the enemies are.

To get your colleagues to hang together, remind them that the enemy is the competition. The enemy is never having enough time to do the work. The enemy is whatever stands in the way of making great work.

Remind your colleagues that you need one another to create the best possible advertising in the most efficient and cost-effective way. Remind them you are smarter together than you are alone.

Above all, remind them that if you don't hang together and help one another, you will hang separately, soon after the client replaces your agency with another.

37

Judgment Overrides Any Rule

Martin Puris, co-founder and former CEO of the great agency Ammirati & Puris, has said,

> The job of account executive is the most difficult in the agency business. It's an intellectual high-wire act.

> The two fatal mistakes an account person can make are to become either the client's "man" at the agency—or the agency's "man" at the client.

> Both fail.

> A good account person gives us objectivity, commitment, insight, and—above all—truth.

Martin is not an account person. He is a writer, famed for having penned "The Ultimate Driving Machine" for automaker BMW, but here he is saying the job of an Account Executive is "the most difficult in the agency business." In this he shares a view with former Ogilvy Chair Shelly Lazarus, who you'll recall asked, "It seems so simple. Why is it so hard?"

So, why is it so hard?

It is no small challenge to counterbalance client demands with agency realities, and to manage money and time when both have become increasingly scarce. An even bigger challenge is to have the judgment needed to do and say exactly the right thing in exactly the right way to exactly the right person at exactly the right time.

Some account people seem to have great instincts about this. But I'll bet if you look deeper, you'll find that there's more to their judgment skills than just good instincts. I'll bet you'll find that the account people with the best judgment are the ones who made mistakes and learned from them. Their good judgment comes in part from previous bad judgment.

This is a book of rules, but an account executive works in a world of *exceptions*. No rule can accommodate every situation, and no list of rules is exhaustive. In the end, the only rule you can rely on is this: judgment rules.

38

Ideas Are the Currency
We Trade in

"I think you'll like this idea—it's sort of 'dull' meets 'inoffensive.'"

Look at any great agency—in emerging or traditional forms of communication—and what you will find in common is the ability to formulate enduring ideas that appeal to countless people striving for whatever it is they aspire to.

I think of agencies like Wieden + Kennedy and its *Just Do It* work for Nike. Or TBWA\Chiat\Day and its *1984* commercial and its *Think Different* campaign for Apple. Or Goodby Silverstein and *Got Milk*. Even my own former shop, Ammirati & Puris, gained well-deserved praise for its famous *Ultimate Driving Machine* advertising for BMW.

These shops and many, many others—of all sizes, in varied specialties, here in the United States and around the world—will gladly show you a select number of ads that garner respect and admiration. Every reasonably decent shop has at least a few of these.

But peel away the layers of self-promotion and hyperbole, and what you will find are ads and campaigns that are truly great in alarmingly short supply. That's because generating great ideas is hard, really, *really* hard.

Ideas are the currency we trade in. They distinguish subpar agencies from average ones, average ones from good ones, and good ones from the few truly great ones. Ideas are prized by clients, celebrated by writers and art directors, feared by competitors. Everyone wants to work at an agency known for creating great ideas. But not every agency is routinely up to the task.

So how do we create more great ideas?

One possible answer is to hire more great people, the true geniuses—the few, the wild, the possibly crazy—who are able to generate one great idea after another. The problem is, genius is a scarce resource, not just in advertising, but in every other creative endeavor you can imagine. Relying on genius seems, at least to me, like playing a losing hand.

Another option lies in methodologies you can follow, brainstorming techniques you can use, or even books you can read, each promoting their own version of idea formulating wizardry. Everyone has their theories. Some might work, many don't, but all of them at least *sound* convincing.

OCCAM'S RAZOR

I, too, have a theory. It is not original with me—credit is due its inventor, a fourteenth-century theologian and philosopher named William of Occam—but the one thing I can say is, it *does* work more often than not.

William of Occam is the creator of "Occam's Razor," a principle that says, "The simplest explanation is usually the correct one."

Simple is better. By extension, simple is better in formulating ideas.

There is something appealingly elegant and enticing with a theory that suggests that the solution lies in simplicity. But let's say you're a skeptic. Maybe you don't trust a figure from the dark, remote, and inaccessible Middle Ages. So how about someone more contemporary, like Steve Jobs maybe?

Here is what Jobs says about the subject: "Simple can be harder than complex: you have to work hard to get your thinking clean and make it simple. But it's worth it in the end because once you get there, you can move mountains."

So now we have William of Occam and Steve Jobs. Still not convinced? Let's add Richard Branson to the mix: "Complexity is your enemy. Any fool can make something complicated. It is hard to make something simple."

Okay, now we have William of Occam, Steve Jobs, *and* Richard Branson. For me, this is more than enough evidence of the virtues of simplicity, but perhaps not for you, so how about an example of "simple is better," taken not from the advertising business, but instead from the entertainment industry? The subject is the famous and highly regarded Hollywood producer Jerry Weintraub, covering an incident he had while representing Elvis Presley.

Weintraub's agreement with Presley's management was that the star would never play to anything other than a sold-out house. Location didn't matter; venue didn't matter; day of the week didn't matter; *every* show had to be sold out.

Weintraub booked Presley to perform two shows at a venue, one a matinee, followed by an evening show. The day before the two shows were scheduled to run, Weintraub discovered the matinee was not sold out, violating his contract.

So what does Weintraub do? He has 5,000 unsold tickets for the matinee. With just 24 hours before the show, how does he sell those 5,000 empty seats?

The answer is: he *doesn't*. Instead, he arranges to have those 5,000 seats *removed* for the matinee, then restored for the evening performance.

Most of us would have scrambled to figure out how to sell those seats. And most of us surely would have failed. Weintraub looked at this problem in a different but astonishingly simple and elegant way to arrive at a solution. How many of us would have thought to remove seats from the venue?

How about another example, one all of us have experienced first-hand, and likely more than once if you have had occasion to board a commercial airline. Assuming you have, do you ever recall being delayed?

I thought so.

For years, airlines have grappled with their inability to land planes on time, as scheduled. How do they deal with this? Do they reconfigure air traffic control, upgrade their computer systems, or reorient their logistics to improve on-time performance?

They do *none* of these things. Instead, they do something far simpler to address the problem: they don't look to technology or logistics for the solution; they look to their printing company.

The airlines reconfigure their flight schedules, allotting more time for each flight than they normally need. So, for example, a flight from San Francisco should take about five and a half hours; they allow six. The result: more planes arrive on time, not because they are performing better, but because the schedules are more forgiving.

In retrospect, this seems like an obvious solution. But if I imagine myself confronting the problem, I would think in terms of the hard stuff—systems, technology, logistics—not the easy stuff, like adjusting the schedules.

This is another brilliant example of simplicity at work.

These two stories admittedly aren't about advertising, but the core principle holds true. If you apply the principle to the best advertising and marketing, the work that has endured, you likely will see it is driven by simple, powerful ideas.

THAT QUESTION AGAIN

That's great, but what happens when great ideas remain stubbornly out of reach, not readily forthcoming? Here's another approach: instead of thinking of answers, think of questions. Ask, "Why can't we try X?" Or, "What if we tried Y?"

A simple, perfectly framed question often can lead to a brilliant idea. Let me give you an example: many of you know the name Eddie Bauer, the famous outdoorsman and founder of the stores that bear his name.

I have no idea if this conversation actually happened, but let's imagine Bauer one day asked a "why" question, as in, "Why don't more people try our products?," followed by a "what if" question, as in, "What if we could make them more confident in their purchases?" These "why" and "what if" questions led to the creation of *The Unconditional Guarantee.*

Shop at an Amazon, Zappos, Lands' End, L.L. Bean, or one of a seemingly infinite number of retailers and you will see the unconditional guarantee at work. Retailers offering the guarantee are the rule; those not offering the guarantee are the exception. The Unconditional Guarantee utterly changed the face of retailing as we know it.

Any retailer that wants to express confidence in the products they sell will turn to Eddie Bauer's guarantee as evidence. It says, in essence, "We are confident in what we're offering, and are prepared to stand behind it." In fact, Bauer himself said, *"My greatest contribution to the consumer was our 100% unconditional lifetime guarantee. That guarantee was part of what I sold."*

Okay, maybe you don't care about retail, or maybe you don't care about Eddie Bauer, or maybe you're suspicious of the imaginary conversation I created to demonstrate the validity of the "why" and "what if" questions. How about another example, this one not imagined, but very real, one in which I was a participant?

I was meeting with my colleagues at Digitas, including the agency's founder, Michael Bronner. Our task was to formulate a new and better way to conduct a frequent-user loyalty program for one of our clients.

We were kicking around all sorts of ideas, some preposterous, others boring, and still others irrelevant. Michael then asked a seemingly simple "why" question: "Why do frequent flyer programs have to be limited to a single airline?"

I followed that question with a "what if" question: "Well, Michael, what if we created a program that included lots of airlines?"

At first we were about to discard this idea as stupid, but as we thought about it, we realized this might be the path to something new, even groundbreaking. At the time, no other company had a program such as this with multiple participants.

We continued to work through the idea, including all the obvious obstacles, particularly how we convince what are fierce competitors to cooperate with one another in a program that serves all their respective interests.

We found means to address these issues, and once we did, took our idea to the folks at the charge card company that was our client, meeting with their Gold and Platinum Card divisions, which were led by a young, enormously impressive executive.

The company is American Express, one of the world's stellar brands. The executive is Ken Chenault, one of the world's most accomplished CEOs. The program was *Membership Miles*, which ultimately evolved into *Membership Rewards*, which continues to this day, and is, by any estimation, among the world's most effective loyalty programs for consumers, and utterly key to American Express's growth, success, and brand equity.

Unlike the imagined Eddie Bauer example, the American Express example really happened, with an outcome well beyond anyone's ambitions.

Think about your own experience: how many times did a question lead to an insight that led to an idea? I'm guessing this occurs more frequently than you might realize. And this, along with William of Occam's "simple is better" principle, is another way to attempt addressing the daunting challenge of formulating great ideas.

A while back, I received an email from a young account person named Matt Singer. In our exchange about the previous edition of *The Art of Client Service*, Matt asked, "Out of curiosity, if you had to choose only one piece in there [the book] of advice for a 24-year-old account guy to really pay attention, what do you think it would be?"

Putting aside for the moment Matt's tortured syntax (sorry, Matt), *The Art of Client Service* includes one piece of advice after another, but Matt was asking me to single out one. How do I do this? It's a losing proposition if ever there was one.

The answer I gave didn't actually come from that book. It is instead something I've been thinking about for some time. Here's what I said: "One is really hard, but if I think back on all my years as a line account guy, and reflect on the thousands of conversations I've had with clients, colleagues, and competitors, I would say the one thing that matters is *knowing how to ask the right question.*"

Know how to ask the right question. Why is this so important?

To me, knowing how to ask the right question says you're smart, you really listen, and demonstrates your skill as a communicator.

When I say this and people respond with a questioning look, or worse, I tend to quote author Malcolm Gladwell, who, when he was interviewed on the television show *60 Minutes*, said, "I think the really obvious questions are the great ones."

I am in violent agreement with this. The fact is, embedded in every perfectly framed question is an idea waiting to reveal itself.

THE POWER OF OBSERVATION

Okay, by now I might have bludgeoned you into submission about the importance of keeping things simple as you formulate ideas—remember Occam's Razor, Steve Jobs, and Richard

Branson—and to think in terms of "why" and "what if" questions when inspiration fails you. But what if you still come up empty? There's a third approach I'd like to share, best illustrated by a story.

There's an agency that once worked with a company in the wireless telecommunications business. After the agency won the account, the client briefed them on the business, telling them they determined their target audience to mainly be higher income, white collar professionals.

The agency easily could have accepted this as fact and proceeded to work on strategy and creative, but instead decided to examine this for themselves. They asked for and received permission to set up shop in a selection of retail locations where the service was sold.

The agency set up shop in store after store, observing consumers, noting the questions they asked, and watching how they transacted business. Two weeks later, they arrived at a simple but powerful insight: the client was missing its market!

Instead of having higher income professionals as its market, the client actually was serving lower income, blue collar people who essentially were living paycheck to paycheck. This insight—the product of simple observation—led to a radical shift in the creative and media approach the agency recommended and the client accepted, leading to a huge increase in performance.

You would think this kind of sophisticated performance was done on behalf of an industry leader like Verizon or T-Mobile. It wasn't. The client was a small Midwestern firm called Einstein Wireless.

If you guessed the agency would be equally sophisticated—an Ideo or R/GA—you would be wrong again. The firm was O'Berry Collaborative. And no, they are not located in New York or Los Angeles. They are in Bozeman. Yes, that Bozeman, in Montana.

The point: observation leads to insight. You don't have to be an Ideo or an R/GA working for a Verizon or a T-Mobile to master this underlying principle.

So now we have three ways to create more ideas: (1) the potency of simplicity; (2) the perfectly framed questions that lead to an idea; and (3) the power of observation.

━━━━━━

DISCIPLINE, ACCIDENTS, AND IDEA FORMATION

There are two more thoughts I'd like to share with you. For these, I have Charlie Rose to thank. Rose, as many of you know, hosts the nightly PBS *Charlie Rose* show, where he interviews famous and not-so-famous people—writers, reporters, directors, actors, musicians, politicians, maybe me some day (one can hope)—that has a relatively small but intensely influential, loyal group of viewers. One evening he interviewed the actor Jake Gyllenhaal, who appeared to promote his then just-released movie, *Nightcrawler*. Gyllenhaal, Dan Gilroy—the movie's director, who also appeared on the show—and Rose go through what felt like a typical "call and response" exchange, until there's a moment when Gyllenhaal says, "Freedom is on the other side of discipline." Rose, never at a loss for words, is stopped in his tracks by this remark, so stunned is he by this pronouncement from an actor who claims it is *preparing* for a role, not acting in a role, that he finds most enticing.

Soon thereafter, Rose has another conversation, this time with another actor, Dame Helen Mirren, who was in town to promote her appearance as Queen Elizabeth in the Broadway show *The Audience*. Again, some back and forth between Rose and Mirren, until there's a moment when Mirren says, in her perfectly precise English accent, "… accident is very important in art, but you can only achieve accident in a full way after you've fully mastered technique."

For those of us not actors, but still striving for that next great idea, there are two takeaways from Gyllenhaal and Mirren: the liberating necessity of discipline and technique to the creative process and the role *accident* plays in idea formation.

What, exactly, does Gyllenhaal mean by "discipline and technique"? To me, they mean full-on preparation, deep knowledge, and thorough understanding of the subject at hand. They mean the more you are in control of your craft—in their words, "discipline and technique"—the more likely that next idea will emanate from you.

Equally important, Mirren suggests you likely won't create that next great idea sitting in your office, at your desk. You might just as easily create that idea in a time and place where you least expect it—taking a run, doing yoga, even in, yes, the shower—and need to be open and available to the epiphany when it strikes.

I don't know about all of you, but for seven years I was a dedicated watcher of the AMC television program *Mad Men*. In the final season, in the final episode of the show, in the final scene, there is a shot of the show's protagonist, Don Draper (played by the actor Jon Hamm), at an Esalen-style retreat, sitting cross-legged, high above the California coastline, the ocean serving as a backdrop. Don is meditating. The slightest smile of knowing inspiration appears on his face. Immediately thereafter, the scene cuts to Coca-Cola's famed *Hilltop* commercial, driven by the jingle, "I'd like to buy the world a Coke and keep it company."

In post-finale interviews, *Mad Men* creator and showrunner Matthew Weiner admits he intended viewers to make the connection, tying Draper to the creation of the famous commercial, ending the show by validating his role as a kind of creative advertising genius.

But that's fiction, you say. You're right. What actually happened in real life?

There was a story in *The New York Times*, called "Behind a '71 Coke Jingle, A Man Who Wasn't Mad." It speaks of a creative person name Bill Backer, who later would found the agency Backer and Spielvogel, but at the moment was working as a writer for Coca-Cola's advertising agency, McCann Erickson. Backer tells a story of being on a flight to London when, due to fog, it was unexpectedly diverted to an airport in Shannon, Ireland. The airport waiting area was cramped; people were angry. But Backer noticed that as people milled around, talking with one another, sharing bottles of Coca-Cola, their anger seemed to dissipate. This is when the line came to him: on a napkin he wrote the now famous words, "I'd like to buy the world a Coke and keep it company...." That was the beginning of a now legendary commercial.

This could be art imitating life, or life imitating art; either way, it drives home Mirren's point about "accident in art."

So important are ideas to advertising's very survival, we spend countless hours seeking them, formulating them, anguishing about them. I am certain you have techniques to add to the ones I've shared, but let me recap these five for you:

1. Follow William of Occam's rule of **simple**.

2. Frame the issue with "why" and "what if" **questions**.

3. Use **observation** to lead to insights to drive strategy, creative, and media.

4. Understand "Freedom is the other side of discipline" to gain **mastery** of your craft.

5. Give license to the power of **serendipity**.

I'm an account person. Conventional wisdom says I should have no ideas. To this I say, "The hell with convention wisdom!" Ideas can come at any time, from anywhere, from anyone, including me, and, of course, you.

With that, I'd love to end this chapter right here. But the reality is, you might try any or all of techniques and *still* come up dry. What do you do then? Do you simply give in?

You do not.

There is a saying, "there are no new ideas." If this is true, and if you happen to buy in to this even slightly, then my suggestion is you look at the work of others to see if you can jumpstart your own eureka, smack-the-head moment. To help, what follows are three examples of great work that might spark an idea of your own.

APPLE'S *1984*

Most of us remember the commercial Apple Computer made, called *1984*, largely because it is almost universally recognized as the most famous television commercial in advertising history.

The making of that commercial has been widely reported. After viewing the spot, Apple's board of directors were mystified by it. "There's no product!" they said. Many were fiercely opposed to running it as a Super Bowl commercial, which is what was proposed.

Opposition was so intense that Apple's two founders, Steve Jobs and Steve Wozniak, offered to pay out of their own pockets the $500,000 needed to run the spot. (In an era when Super Bowl 30-second spots cost around $4 million, it can be hard to believe commercials on America's biggest TV spectacle could be had for *just* $500,000.)

In the end, the board relented, the spot ran, and the rest is advertising history.

But in thinking about the offer made by the two Steves, I could only conclude they believed in the advertising, as radical as it must have seemed to them, because they believed in another Steve, Steve Hayden, and in Lee Clow, the Chiat\Day creative leaders responsible for making it.

In short, the advertising took great risks in its creation, which was radical, and in its running, which was financial. It ran because of the trust and faith Apple's founders had in their agency. It became great advertising, countering the conventions of the day, because it was driven by a powerful, simple idea—according to Steve Hayden, it was not fear of IBM. Instead, it was the "collective fear of technology"—that consumers could embrace and rally to, proving that there's more to a technology commercial than product, price, and features.

Was it great advertising? We remember it to this day, so yes, in that sense it was great. Did it sell more Apple Macintoshes? That I doubt. How do you buy something when you don't know what it costs, what it has to offer, and why it's better than its alternatives? But it clearly made consumers take notice, it generated enormous buzz, and it paved the way for the introduction of something new, different, and potentially better. So yes, in that sense, it was more than just a 30-second TV commercial with a great backstory. It was great advertising.

PUPPY LOVE AND LOST DOG

Even if I didn't own two dogs that I love as family, I still would be drawn to the Budweiser puppy commercials that ran during a couple of recent Super Bowls.

Each is an amazing piece of storytelling, backed by terrific acting, great direction, beautiful cinematography, and perfectly chosen music, all in support of a lovable Labrador puppy who pulls you into the narrative.

But, again, like Apple's *1984*, is it good advertising? I am nowhere close to matching Budweiser's target audience—too old, too focused on other alcoholic beverages, too cognizant of advertising's bald attempt at manipulating my emotions—but even so, I am not completely immune to the commercials' charms.

The fact is, I love the stories, don't understand the advertising, and, unlike Apple—a company I admire—I have no time for Anheuser-Busch. I would never drink their beer, even if came gushing free from my kitchen spigot. The commercials, as entertaining as they are, do nothing to alter my view, and certainly don't prompt me to go to the store for a six-pack of what is considered by many to be little more than piss-water.

But how can you not love that adorable lab puppy, a pal and beneficiary of a rescue by the Clydesdale horses—the true heroes of the advertising—the enduring symbols of the Anheuser-Busch brand? And, again, clearly I am not the target of the advertising, so what I think of the product is largely irrelevant. And everyone remembers the commercials and associates Budweiser with them.

Those in the target audience surely must have been drawn to the story. Who wouldn't be?

LIFE GOES ON

Advertising icon David Ogilvy once said, "Nobody should be allowed to create general advertising until he's served his apprenticeship in direct response." For Ogilvy, advertising was about selling, not entertaining.

David Ogilvy is inadvertently right about general advertising: there is too much entertaining, and not enough selling. You certainly could argue that Apple's *1984* and Budweiser's *Puppy Love* and *Lost Puppy* are guilty of too much entertainment, and short on selling.

David Ogilvy also is right about direct marketing, but not in the way I suspect he intended: with Direct, there is too much selling, and not enough entertaining. The problem with most direct response advertising is this: it's crap. Too much price, too much product, too much promotion, not enough story.

But why can't we make advertising that does both, that sells and entertains? There's an example of such advertising that I want to share with you, a television spot made for insurance.

Insurance is a low-involvement category for products no one wants to think about, and yet here we have Flo for Progressive, Mayhem for Allstate, and the Gecko for GEICO. The product might be boring; the advertising surely is not.

But a far less glamorous side to the business is the part dealing with life insurance promoted by direct response television advertising (DRTV). Here the task is not to entertain you with Charlie Brown or an animated lizard with a British accent, but rather to get you to respond. The budgets are far smaller, with the challenge far larger, given how much is riding on that response.

The agency Womenkind was charged with such an assignment recently: make advertising for Mutual of Omaha, a client new to DRTV. Their assignment: craft commercials that stand out, connect with consumers, and make the phone ring, without a budget to afford union acting talent, let alone a celebrity spokesperson.

This is the point at which most agencies give in, and do more of the same predictable stuff you see from other agencies. Not Womenkind. Instead, the agency discovered and tapped into a surprisingly simple, yet profound, insight about selling life insurance.

Competitors focused on the front end of the transaction: the cost and ease of application. What if Womenkind focused on the back-end, telling people about the high percentage of claims the company paid, and how quickly? Nobody talks about stuff like this, but there was a realization of how truly important these things are.

The commercials that resulted promoted these benefits. The results were beyond expectation. Not only did we meet our numbers, we exceeded the target by a healthy 15 percent, with brand building advertising that is unlike any other on the air.

If you have a chance check out *Life Goes on* at the Womenkind website or on YouTube, you'll see why it works: great stories, well told, with solid acting performances, great music, well-made production values. It does an extraordinary job of turning a tragedy into something life affirming, without ever devolving into the maudlin, all the while staying focused on the task at hand: encourage consumers to pick up the phone and call. Listen closely to the script. You'll get a sense of real mastery here.

This spot will never make *Advertising Age*'s "best ads" list, or likely get any sort of recognition, but my view is the achievement is truly worth noting. All driven by asking two simple questions, a "why" and a "what if":

- Why does all direct response advertising have to sound the same?

- What if we did advertising that focused not on the front end of applying for insurance, but instead on the back end, when it comes time to redeem your coverage?

Life Goes on does what David Ogilvy would insist it do: sell. But it also entertains, in a way that is balanced, genuine, and true. And if David Ogilvy were here today to view the spot, I suspect he might proclaim it as a small piece of advertising genius, regardless of what others think.

I learned about brand advertising during my stint at Ammirati & Puris, where we developed *The Ultimate Driving Machine* for BMW, making it clear that performance is the only thing that should command a price premium; and where we developed *The Tightest Ship in the Shipping Business* for UPS, explaining the reason UPS is a less expensive choice than FedEx is because the company is more efficient, and thus can pass to its customers the savings it achieves; and where we developed *The Antidote for Civilization* for Club Med, transforming a lack of phones and televisions in visitors' rooms into something to celebrate, not an obstacle to overcome.

Ammirati made these campaigns, and others like them, to not only entertain viewers, but also to inform them, and to encourage them to act. Did they work?

The Ultimate Driving Machine has been BMW's tagline for nearly 40 years. *The Tightest Ship in the Shipping Business* helped UPS emerge from an overnight package delivery afterthought into a serious contender. And *The Antidote for Civilization* put Club Med on the map as a luxury vacation escape. So yes, I'd say they worked.

Advertising has just three roles to play: (1) create awareness, (2) influence behavior, and (3) get people to buy your stuff. *Puppy Love* and its successor spot *Lost Dog* are great stories, as is *1984*, but all of them fall short on the most important thing: getting people to buy your stuff. If you were to ask which of these three examples is representative of great advertising, I would respond by saying you already know the answer.

But let's not lose sight of the larger point: when Occam's Razor or any of the other techniques fail you, you always can look at the work of others for inspiration. And embedded in that foray into the work of others often will be that bit of genius you're searching for, the thing that clients want most: a great idea.

Part Seven

BUILDING LONG-TERM
CLIENT RELATIONSHIPS

39

Make No Commitment without Consultation

As a young account executive starting out in the business, I had the good fortune to work with the client from hell. I don't know if this client hated agencies in general, or simply hated me in particular, but it seemed as if I could do no right.

I dreaded telephone calls from this client. I would flinch before picking up the phone. Meetings were worse. I'd lie awake the night before in dread.

I remember one particularly difficult discussion about a schedule. The client was biting: "It takes you guys longer to write an ad than it took Tolstoy to write *War and Peace*. I want to see copy two days from now, not two weeks from now. Okay?"

I didn't know it at the time, but this was a test. I was intimidated by this client. When he said, "Okay?" it was strictly rhetorical. He meant, "Get it done, you worthless bag carrier!"

The easy way out would have been to say, "You got it!" and beat a hasty retreat, but I knew that would only delay worse pain. There was no way we could have copy to him in two days, and when we failed to deliver, all the client's rage would be visited on me.

I also knew that saying "no" would mean a meltdown right then and there. He'd pick up the phone, call my boss, and scream at her.

So, in an instant, I said, "Let me make a quick call and see what we can do." The client looked at me derisively. "Sure, go ahead and call your pals." I stepped out of his office, found a phone, and spoke with my creative colleagues. After I did some begging and pleading, they agreed to have something to the client in four days.

I went back to the client and said, "I know you want it in two days, but how about four days? That's a big improvement over two weeks."

His answer: "Three days." To which I replied, "Jerry, I can push the creatives to three days, but it isn't enough time to get the work right. We'll wind up having to do a major rewrite and take even more time. Give us the four days and we'll nail it."

"It better be brilliant," was his reply.

When I got back to the agency, the creatives weren't happy, but they knew what I was dealing with in this client, and they understood. They delivered in four days.

I didn't have an entirely happy client. I didn't have an entirely happy group of colleagues. But I had managed to broker a solution without the client asking my boss to fire me, and without my colleagues thinking I had sold them down the river.

What I took away from this experience is to make no commitment without consultation.

When a client makes a request, let alone a demand, your first, and understandable, instinct is to say yes. The more senior the client, the more urgent the need, the more strident the tone, the more you want to comply on the spot.

Do not do this. Seriously. I mean it. *Do not do this*. You almost surely will regret it.

Even with seemingly simple requests, a unilateral yes is *not* the right answer. It does a terrible disservice to everyone—your colleagues, yourself, and most of all, your client.

A commitment without consultation ignores the collaborative nature of making advertising. It pays no respect to the people you work with. Besides, you might not be able to deliver on your commitment.

You may be a big fish in the agency food chain. You may have the power to say yes, but you and your client will soon feel the consequences of the unchecked exercise of that power. It will undermine teamwork, erode morale, and destroy your credibility.

The fact is, the more senior you are, the easier it is to explain to your client that you need to check with others before saying yes.

That doesn't mean you say no either. Your job is to build bridges, not barriers. *No* is a barrier builder.

So, even when a client makes a seemingly unreasonable request—about a deadline, a budget, a change in the work—*no* is not the right answer. *No* helps no one—not the agency, not your colleagues, and, of course, not the client.

What is the right answer?

When an unqualified yes isn't possible, offer a qualified one: "Here's what we can do. It's not a perfect solution, but does it address your need?"

Discuss, negotiate, collaborate, solve the problem together. Even difficult clients will usually accept a reasonable solution, especially when you've made every effort to give them what they want.

That's what happened with my "client from hell." I admit it wasn't much of a negotiation, but I did get him to accept—yes, grudgingly, derisively, dismissively—a solution a little short of his demand, without completely upsetting my colleagues.

I also lived to work another day.

40

Take on the Coloration of Your Clients; Do Not Compromise Your Character

Some of my clients seem to live for golf. They don't just play it, they breathe it. I don't play golf, but I can talk it. I make a point to read the sports reporting on major golf tournaments. That way, if my clients want to talk about how Jordan Spieth or Rory McIlroy took the golfing world by storm, I'll be ready.

I'm also ready to talk about the latest movie, the hottest Broadway show, or some new restaurant everyone is raving about. From bowling to Beethoven, it doesn't matter. If you're going to be good at account work, you need to be interested in whatever your client is interested in. That means being a voracious consumer of popular culture, and at least on passing terms with higher-brow pursuits.

You also need to be wise enough to sidestep discussions of politics, religion, or controversial subjects best avoided. No matter how friendly you become, remember that clients are still clients, not friends, and edit yourself accordingly.

Client service requires you to be flexible, open-minded, and able to handle the unexpected with grace. It also requires you to never compromise your integrity, honesty, or sense of fairness.

Be a good listener. Take a sincere interest in your clients' lives—professionally and personally—while remaining respectful of their privacy. Don't force the relationship. Take the time needed to build a personal connection.

I worked with two clients for more than a year and got to know them fairly well. We had more than the occasional lunch together. One day, after finishing up a meeting, I suggested the three of us continue the discussion over dinner. Then I remembered that each had a young child. I was a single guy at the time with not much interest in children, but that didn't stop me from suggesting we bring the kids with us.

The five of us went out for pizza. It was as much fun as I've had at any client dinner, and it was a great way to bond with my clients. Every time thereafter, I could ask about their boys by name.

It was a great lesson in taking on the coloration of my clients.

41

Never Forget
It's a Business

I once had one martini too many (two actually, which for a lightweight like me is one too many) over dinner with a client. I wound up saying something I shouldn't have said. Fortunately for me, and my agency, there was no damage as a result. But I learned an important lesson about self-restraint.

If you work with clients long enough, you usually have an opportunity to spend time with them outside the office. There's the occasional lunch or dinner. You might play golf or tennis together, or go to a ballgame. These are good things to do. Spending time away from work allows you to talk about work in a different context. You can use such occasions not only to be social, but also to deal with tough issues.

No matter how many dinners you attend, no matter how friendly you become with your client, never mistake your relationship for personal friendship. Never forget that the person sitting across from you is always your client.

So watch what you drink, watch how you behave, and watch what you say. No tales out of school, no "that's the alcohol talking" disclosures you will live to regret the morning after.

42

Once a Client,
Always a Client

I exchanged emails the other day with a client. Not a current client. I haven't worked with this individual in more than a dozen years, but I've made it a point to stay in touch. After this passage of time, it's looking pretty unlikely that we'll ever get to work together again. It doesn't matter.

Once a client and I are no longer working together, I don't decide to stay in touch based on how likely that client is to run a big account again. My view is that once you've been my client, you'll *always* be my client.

If you're my client and are open to staying in contact after we're no longer working together, I'll make sure we do. If there's a way I can be of help, I'll do my best.

That client with whom I was in contact reads my blog. He's served as a job reference. He's recommended me to possible clients and potential employers. I've done much the same for him.

As I said, he's not likely to be my client again, but that is beside the point. He's my friend.

43

Going Rogue

You've probably read about top account people who develop such a close personal relationship with their clients that they are said to "own" the account. In truly extreme cases, an account person can shop the client to competing agencies. If the account person switches agencies, the client switches with them.

I can't begin to say how completely, utterly unethical this is. Yes, one of your mandates is to forge a strong bond with your client. Yes, people work with people, not with organizations. But this does not give you license to ignore your obligations to the agency that employs you. This is the primary reason agencies now make senior executives sign non-solicit, non-compete agreements that are designed to prevent account people from taking clients with them when they switch agencies.

Your job is to build a strong client relationship on behalf of your *agency*, not on behalf of yourself. You do not own the client relationship. You are merely the keeper of it. You have a fiduciary and an ethical responsibility to do everything in your power to ensure that the client feels loyal not just to you, but to other people in the agency, and to the agency as a whole.

If you have done your best to facilitate ties between your client and the agency, the client is much less likely to go with you if you change agencies. If the client does decide to find a new agency after you've left, you'll know that it wasn't due to any shortcoming on your part, but rather on a shortcoming at the shop you left behind. You'll be known as a person of integrity.

In the context of a long career, that is far more valuable than any short-term gain you might derive from "going rogue" with an account that you should leave behind when you trade your current agency for a new one.

Part Eight

HOW TO DEAL WITH UNHAPPY CLIENTS

44

Always Think Endgame

"No, Thursday's out. How about never—is never good for you?"

The client was wrong. The agency had agreed to create a print ad on a ridiculously tight schedule, with the understanding that we would do our creative presentation on a particular day. Now the client was saying she couldn't meet on the day we had agreed to. She wanted to delay a day, but still make all the magazine closings. "You can make up the day in the schedule," she said.

Normally we could. Normally we would be delighted to have an extra day to develop creative concepts. But this schedule wasn't normal. It was broken down into hours, not days. A day lost was a big deal. It threatened to blow our closing dates.

We could have insisted on holding to the original schedule. We could have won the argument, but we would have lost in the end.

The client would remember. The next time we needed her to be flexible on a date, I could see her pointing to the schedule, then pointing to me and saying, "This is what you committed to, so don't even think about asking for an extra hour, let alone an extra day."

So we figured out how to make the publication closings, even with the one-day delay on the creative presentation. The message: working with clients and colleagues is a never-ending process of negotiation and compromise. Always think endgame. Remember that an argument won can become an account lost.

45

No Surprises about Money or Time

After I took over running a major account at one of the agencies I worked for, I discovered the agency had, during a period of seven months, exceeded the agreed-on fee budget by nearly $1 million. Yes, that's right: One million dollars.

The client/agency relationship had been rocky, and the previous leadership on the account chose not to disclose the fee overrun to the client, fearing it would jeopardize the account.

I inherited this problem knowing that a cardinal rule of account service is to never surprise your clients about a cost overrun or a scheduling delay. But I had the advantage of being the new guy on the account. I investigated the cost overrun. It appeared that roughly half of it was due to agency inefficiency, the other half due to excessive client changes and unbudgeted additional assignments.

When the client made revisions to the work and added assignments, the agency, of course, should have adjusted its budgets and secured client approval for higher fees. The agency, fearing for the future of the account, failed to do this. Over time, as the problem grew larger and larger, it became increasingly difficult to address. Rather than bringing up the issue with the client, the account team ignored it. When the agency's accounting department pressed the account team to speak with the client, the account people responded, "If we do, we'll lose the account!"

I told my management that I was going to settle the issue without delay. I prepared them to expect nothing better than half of the $1 million overage. Then I went to see the client. I took her through the problem, apologized for the agency's failure to disclose it, offered to have the agency absorb half the overage, and assured them it would never happen again.

Instead of being angry, which she had every right to be, and instead of firing the agency on the spot, which she easily could have done, the client accepted my apology and my solution. We went on to have a very productive relationship for years thereafter.

This was a problem not of my own making, but even so, I vowed I would never be placed in that position again. I made a commitment to myself that I would always advise clients up front about the expense and timing implications of their decisions, so they could make fully informed decisions.

When a client calls with a change or a request, it can make you feel a little uncomfortable to say, "Let me figure out what the change will cost and if it will have an impact on the schedule, then get right back to you."

But you owe it to your clients, and to your agency, to do exactly that. By doing so, you avoid the perils of "scope creep," when a project grows beyond what initially was planned. And you avoid any after-the-fact surprises that result in painful consequences, ranging from a loss of money, to a loss of trust, to a lost account.

46

Deal with Problems Head-On

Advertising is people intensive. Given the number of hands that touch even the simplest assignment, it is astonishing how much work gets produced error-free. Still, things get derailed. On occasion, there is a full-scale train wreck. A deadline gets blown. There is a mistake in a print ad. The wrong commercial gets shipped.

When something goes awry, get to your client with a full explanation of what happened and why. Whenever possible, be prepared to outline one or more ways to address the problem. Move quickly. You want to deliver the bad news to the clients. You don't want them to hear it from another source.

If the agency is on the hook for serious money, get senior management involved immediately and work out what you are prepared to do financially before you call the client. Volunteer the financial solution before the client asks for it.

Above all, never, ever lie to your client. Sure, you might get away with it this time. At some point, though, you won't. Once you're caught in a lie, your single greatest asset—your credibility—will be gone forever.

47

If Things Go Wrong,
Take the Blame

Years ago, an agency Creative Director and I had lunch with a trade publication reporter. The reporter asked about the work we were doing for one client. The Creative Director explained that we were working on a new product launch for that client. The reporter took note, and a couple of days later the published story on our agency included a reference to the client's product launch.

There was just one small problem: the client had not announced the new product yet.

The client was furious when he called me. He demanded to know how the agency could be so stupid. I explained it was my fault. I didn't say anything about the Creative Director spilling the news. As far as I was concerned, it was my job to make sure the Creative Director didn't reveal anything confidential.

I wasn't the author of the mistake, but I didn't think twice about taking ownership of it.

You provide air cover for everyone in the agency. If something goes wrong in media, in creative, in production, then it happened on your watch. You are responsible. Take ownership, and be prepared to take the heat from the client.

48

What Happens When I Screw Up?

In Chapter 45, I said that when working with clients, there should be absolutely no surprises about money or time. You'll recall that I rode in on the proverbial white horse to rescue my agency from a very difficult financial situation. My solution was actually quite simple—split the dollar difference and learn a lesson—but it saved the agency, and it kept our client. I was pretty proud of myself for being so wise and resourceful.

But enough about this rare occasion of personal competence. Let's talk instead about a more frequent example of when I screwed up. You'll note I didn't say "*if* I screw up." It's "when I screw up" and not "if I screw up" because I have had occasion to screw up often.

The story begins innocently enough. I wrote a direct mail recommendation for a client that included a rough cost estimate and a projected mail quantity. I developed the estimate using a fairly logical set of assumptions based on my years of experience, and I felt I was safe with the number.

My client liked what I presented and gave us approval to proceed. I wrote a creative brief, confirmed a schedule, and briefed the creative team. After some back-and-forth with the writer, art director, and creative director, we arrived at a couple of ideas we liked. We took them to the client. After a few more back-and-forths, we arrived at a plan that pleased all of us.

I then wrote detailed specifications for the idea and put the job out to bid.

The numbers came back. We were over budget. Not by 10 percent, or even 20 percent, which I might have been able to defend. No, as I added up the costs, it became clear that we were over by more than twice the amount I had estimated earlier. Yes, that's right: the actual cost was more than double what I had said the work would cost.

These were not hourly fees that we could absorb, which would be bad enough; these were hard costs due to third parties. It's a good thing the windows didn't open because I might have been inclined to jump.

In truth, going airborne was not an option. I needed another solution. I thought about revising or eliminating some of the pieces that would go in the package. But in the end, it became clear only one thing would truly make an impact: cut the mailing quantity.

I asked our printer to refigure the package at 50 percent of the original press run. To my eternal relief, the numbers came back nearly on target. Although the final mailing would be half the initial estimate, it still would be larger and more ambitious than anything the client had previously attempted. That at least was one positive note in an otherwise grim reality.

Now all I had to do was sell this to the client, but there was one complicating factor: I was scheduled to go out of town the following week, and I wouldn't be able to speak with him face to face. No problem, I thought — I'll write him an email.

I wrote a long, meticulously detailed analysis of the problem, described the various solutions I explored, then offered a solution. Before I pressed "send," I wanted another opinion, so I emailed the document to a colleague for a comment. He wrote back: "You cannot send this email. This problem is too serious, and the solution too complicated, for email. It needs a 'live' discussion."

He was right, of course. It was as if he had read my book and I hadn't. I thought about it for a minute, and decided to reschedule my out-of-town meeting. I then wrote to my client and scheduled a meeting on Monday.

On Monday, I took him through the whole situation: the source of the problem, the possible solutions, and the recommendation. I admit I cringed when he said, "You are actually double the budget? How can that possibly be?" But without further complaint, with no invective, and to his eternal credit, he focused on the problem. He was largely responsible for our working out something satisfactory. It wasn't a happy meeting, but we got done what we needed to get done.

Now I could say this outcome would have been very different had I not gotten to know this client well and had I not developed a measure of trust and mutual respect along the way. But that's not what I'm going to say.

I've been in this business for nearly 30 years and certainly knew better, and yet I still managed to screw up big-time.

The lesson? Do not assume anything, and never, ever, be as glib or as cavalier as I was about money. Check and recheck your claims. Then check them again. Above all, remember your own advice. And by God, make sure you follow it.

49

Getting Fired

Just about everyone who works in advertising and marketing covets a car account. High profile, prestigious, often lucrative, and full of challenges, car accounts compel many an agency to go to great lengths to compete for and win an auto client, which makes Volkswagen's awarding its $400 million business to the agency Crispin, Porter + Bogusky in the mid-2000s without a review even more puzzling until you take a deeper look at the backstory.

Volkswagen had hired Kerry Martin to serve as vice president of marketing and brand innovation. Martin had previously worked with Crispin when she was director of marketing at Mini U.S.A., where she collaborated with the agency on resuscitating a near-dormant brand on a very limited budget. There are lots of reasons why Martin made the change, but among other things, it is a testament to the power of relationships.

That's a tale with a happy ending, except for what happened to Arnold, the agency that fell victim to Martin's decision. It was a situation many of us have faced: an account makes a change in marketing personnel. The new marketing chief wants to make an impact. The easiest way to demonstrate change is to fire the incumbent agency. That's what happened in this case without even going through the motions of a review.

I know first-hand the empty, defeated feeling of losing a client. I was fired by Standard Oil of Ohio. I was fired by Digital Equipment Corporation. I was fired by MasterCard. I was fired by General Motors. I was fired by companies with names so obscure you would not recognize them.

The stated reasons were many—the work was not good enough; the process was broken; the cost was too high—but I think what I was told and what was true diverge. As I look at all of these failures, the thread that connects them all was a breakdown in trust. My clients no longer believed in me and my colleagues. They stopped listening to us, and no longer relied on our counsel.

I once worked with an agency executive who didn't like to travel to the city where one of our largest clients was located. My colleague was a very senior guy, critical to building a relationship with top management. During the years the agency worked with this client, my colleague was an all-too-infrequent presence at the client's headquarters.

The client fired us after some ongoing issues that we couldn't seem to get resolved. There were lots of reasons why we were dismissed. One of them, I think, was a lack of attention from our agency's senior management. The client's CEO found it too easy to fire us because there was no relationship at the top. Perhaps if there had been one, the outcome might have been different.

A client determined to say goodbye usually cannot be deterred, but for those clients with whom even a shred of hope exists, a smart account executive will do all the things outlined in this book to build and sustain trust. It will not make you immune to the often-terminal disease of account loss, but it will make you far less likely to fall ill.

Part Nine

REGAINING CLIENT TRUST

50

How Happy Clients Help You Gain New Ones

A few years back, I went looking for an art director to help me with the PowerPoint presentations I was writing for the workshops I was conducting for clients interested in getting better at client service. I could have relied on a Google search or checked with LinkedIn to find candidates, but did neither. Instead, I called my art director friend and former colleague Sandy Sabean, who put me in touch with Bel Downey. Bel and I have collaborated ever since. If you visit the Acknowledgments section at the end of this book, you will see I thank Bel for having created the cover for this version of *The Art of Client Service*.

When you need a recommendation for a restaurant, or which movie to see, or which music to download, or any other creatively oriented endeavor, you could turn to the web for help, but my sense tells me you turn to your friends and colleagues instead. It is no wonder, then, that for all the media options that clutter the marketing landscape, word-of-mouth referral remains the most powerful form of marketing, and the telephone remains the research tool of choice for many of us.

Which brings me to clients.

Clients have all sorts of options at their disposal when they go shopping for a new agency. They have the web. They have search consultants. They can watch the work of others to see what they like. But the thing I suspect they rely on most is the word of a colleague, a competitor, or a friend. "I need marketing help. Is there an agency you'd recommend I speak with?" has got to be lines spoken by lots of clients seeking someone to collaborate with. If one of your current clients is on the receiving end of a conversation like this, you might well wind up the beneficiary of the discussion: "My shop is doing great work for us. Their people are easy to partner with, and they could help you. You should speak with Jim/Jane Smith. Here's their number. Call them."

What does it take for a scene like this to play out in real life? It takes great ideas combined by nearly flawless execution, performed by people who are all the things this book describes, who are smart, responsive, and nice.

Think what a client referral can mean for your agency. It means you have an immediate connection with a prospective client who is seeking help. It means your work, your process, and you and your colleagues are preapproved. It can greatly foreshorten the new business pitch process. It gives you a distinct advantage over competitors if others are pursuing the same assignment.

If you have clients who like your work, like how you do business, and like and trust you as partners, you still might have to cold-call your way into opportunities, still have to respond to overtures from search consultants, and still have to respond to that random RFI, but I suspect most of your new business wins will come from happy clients who share your name with others.

Happy clients, in short, are the most powerful weapon in new business, which is another reason why happy clients should be the mission of every agency that serves their needs.

It's no wonder that one client referral is worth a thousand cold-call overtures.

51

Five Client Challenges to Agencies

Ask a hundred agency people what's wrong with their shops and you get a hundred different answers.

I'm not a researcher, and what I am about to share is not what you'd technically call *research*. But over the last several years, I've visited a wide range of firms to talk about the challenges they face in dealing with clients and colleagues. And as much as you might expect the answers to vary widely, the reality is, they are remarkably consistent, revolving around five issues:

1. Marketing and advertising agency account people—those charged with overseeing work on behalf of clients—are surprisingly unclear on their roles.

2. A failure to communicate—internally and with clients—is an ongoing concern.

3. There's a need to do a better job of managing client expectations.

4. It's a struggle to get budgets, schedules, and scopes of work consistently right.

5. Clients look to account people for ideas, and are frustrated by their absence.

It didn't matter if the agencies were in New York or from elsewhere. It didn't matter if the shops were large or small. It didn't matter if they were specialized or not. And it didn't matter if they are digitally native or not. The problems identified remain startlingly the same. From the verbatims I received during my hour-long telephone interviews, the highlights of which I share next, it seems as if everyone faces the same obstacles, regardless of circumstances.

———

I. ACCOUNT PEOPLE ARE LARGELY UNCLEAR ON THEIR ROLES

Some people know exactly what their jobs are and what's expected of them, but others do not:

*"'I won't. I can't. That's not in my purview. That's not my job'
seem to be common here. People don't know the job they should
be doing."*

If you're a writer, an art director, or a planner, you know what to do; account people are confused.

*"Everybody defers to everybody else: I don't do social; I don't
do media. Roles and responsibilities aren't clearly defined."*

The best account people define their jobs broadly, filling gaps, doing whatever is needed to support and build the firms they work in. But, judging from the comments I heard, many people do exactly the opposite, defining their jobs narrowly.

*"One of the biggest problems here is that each discipline feels
as if they're doing the other group's job."*

In an environment in which account people don't take charge, others need to step up. The consequence, in the words of one person who put it succinctly, *"Basic account management is
overlooked,"* perhaps because people don't know what *basic* actually entails.

2. A FAILURE TO COMMUNICATE—INTERNALLY AND WITH CLIENTS—IS AN ONGOING CONCERN

Much of the problem has to do with communication, or a lack of it. Advertising and marketing to a large extent are highly collaborative. There are status meetings and conference calls. Copywriters and art directors team up to handle assignments. Problems usually are solved by groups, not individuals. And yet, in the agencies I met with, *"Communication between departments is a problem. We need to have everyone working toward a common goal."*

The fact is, even in an office with an open plan, where it is easy to interact with people, there is a decided preference for email rather than face-to-face communication. To succeed, advertising and marketing require serendipitous contact, where problems get solved and ideas get formulated, yet the ethos is all but abandoned.

"Communication is a BIG thing. There's a lot going on and we need to do a better job to surface issues."

One of the things that became apparent from my conversations with agency people is how little best practices get shared. In case after case, I found people who might solve a particular client problem, but don't take the time to communicate it to others who might benefit.

"There still are silos among teams and functions."

Advertising people typically claim that *clients* are siloed, but the reality is, the agencies that serve them are *equally* siloed, with departments not sharing or connecting with one another.

The consequence of this lack of internal communication is felt acutely by clients who might get an individual's or team's best effort, but rarely gets an entire agency's best effort.

3. THERE'S A NEED TO DO A BETTER JOB OF MANAGING CLIENT EXPECTATIONS

There is not an agency on the planet—okay, perhaps there are a few exceptions—that doesn't suffer one time or another from a failure to manage client expectations. It's a problem everyone struggles with.

"We fail to manage expectations. We let the client manage us."

What seems to suffer the most are basic, take-them-for-granted tasks.

"We need to learn how to communicate with a client about time frames and deadlines, and understanding how to manage expectations."

A failure to manage expectations can have dire consequences for an agency, not just in regard to the clients it serves, but also for the way in which colleagues interact, or fail to interact, with one another.

"We need to set expectations properly. If we don't set those expectations, clients lose faith and trust in us. We also need to manage expectations internally."

A loss of faith and trust is a heavy price to pay for not managing expectations wisely. And yet, the agency people I spoke with are wired to say yes to their clients, no matter how unreasonable the request. So what happens on the occasions when there is no way to say yes? Is the account in jeopardy as a result?

"We need to learn how to say no without putting the business at risk."

The thing clients hate most of all is uncertainty. When an agency doesn't or can't tell them what to expect and why, most clients rebel, with rebellion often taking the form of unreasonable demands, a lose-lose situation for everyone. At the extreme, there's a real risk of losing a client.

---

4. IT'S A STRUGGLE TO GET BUDGETS, SCHEDULES, AND SCOPES OF WORK CONSISTENTLY RIGHT

As much as you might expect clients to be frustrated by a failure to deliver on the big things—strategy and ideas chief among them—it is often the little things that derail a client-agency relationship. There's a budget that's broken, a schedule that sadly misses the mark, or a host of other "minor" irritations occur that slowly accumulate into larger and more meaningful consequences.

"We need to make sure there are no surprises. Clients hate surprises."

There is a nearly universal recognition among agencies that ideas can win a client account, but that a failure to execute can quickly undermine even the best thinking.

"You win business based on creative and strategy, in that order. You lose business based on execution, or lack of it."

There's a well-worn, overused cliché, "God is in the details," that applies here. With so many discrete tasks to execute under increasingly tight deadlines, stuff gets lost.

"We need to teach people how to prevent things from falling through the cracks."

When agency people are running around with their hair on fire, with too much to do and not enough time to do it, even the simplest, most obvious and expected tasks get ignored or overlooked.

"Basic account management is overlooked. For example, a meeting happens, and there's no conference report. There is no accountability."

Agencies that suffer from problems like these often are characterized by a lack of ownership. Instead of having *everyone* step up, *no one* steps up.

"People don't manage schedules properly. There's no sense of ownership."

In more traditional advertising and marketing agencies, it usually fell to account management to define and describe whatever client assignment needed to be formulated and executed, which usually takes the form of a scope of work. But in newer, more digitally native firms, there is often a separation between account management and project management. If these two groups are not on the same page, work doesn't get defined accurately or completely, and things can go off the rails from the outset.

"There's a lack of collaboration between client management and project management. The result is that things don't get scoped properly."

You might think these are things an agency could do in its sleep, do them well, and do them flawlessly. The fact is, they often can't, and usually don't.

5. CLIENTS LOOK TO ACCOUNT PEOPLE FOR IDEAS, AND ARE FRUSTRATED BY THEIR ABSENCE

Even the very best agencies and marketing service firms find it a struggle to come up with that next idea, that next bit of genius. But clients prize ideas, and look to their partners to supply them with increasing regularity, only to be disappointed when reality falls short of expectation.

"We need to bring more strategic ideas to the table, beyond what's expected."

"We haven't been doing new and innovative things; we need to bring new strategies to the table."

With agencies remaining ghetto-ized, with people not in regular communication, and with relationships not being formed as they should be, an agency's ability to collaborate on new thinking is compromised.

"There's no interaction on ideas, no dialogue, which stems from the relationships and the way we cultivate them. We don't have our shit together. It's a bit of a mess."

At some point, agencies lose their way, becoming executors, not thinkers and problem solvers.

"We are more facilitators than strategic marketers."

Each agency brings its owns set of challenges to the clients they deal with, but taking a step back from the particulars, and judging from the numerous conversations I've had with agency personnel at all levels, tenure, and disciplines, I often will find that a lack of job clarity, a failure to communicate, an inability to follow up, shortcomings on things that should be easy, and a paucity of ideas underpin almost every flawed client-agency relationship.

Do agencies recognize how they are falling short? Of course they do. The verbatims are theirs. All of these comments originated with them.

Do clients feel differently? If anything, they might add to the list of issues they're confronting with their agencies, based on their individual circumstances. But it is highly unlikely they would dispute the issues identified here. These problems are chronic and nearly universal. It's the rare firm that avoids any of these.

We are talking about flawed relationships here. Agencies know *what* is wrong. They might even know *why*. So *how* do we fix this?

52

Five Client Service Principles to Believe In

I was in Cleveland not long ago, conducting workshops for a client that acts more like an advertising or marketing agency than the technology company they claim to be, and realized I needed some form of shorthand people could use to guide their actions once they left the presentation room. I am a believer in the rule of three, and started there. Are there three pieces of advice I could leave my audience with?

I couldn't get quite manage this. Three is too hard a number for me. But five pieces of advice work; they are:

1. Show up;
2. Follow up;
3. Speak up;
4. Make it up;
5. Never give up.

Yes, you've heard all of this before, right here, in the pages of this book, but I follow the rule of "Tell them what you're *going* to tell them; tell them; then tell them what you *told* them."

We are at the "told them" part.

SHOW UP

Traveling to see your clients is expensive, hard, and time-consuming. Email is cheap, easy, and fast. Why not email instead of visit, especially when you realize clients are busy, too, and *don't* really want to see you?

This is one case in which I will tell you to ignore your clients' wishes, follow your best intentions, and get on that plane, train, or automobile. Do *not* wait until there is a crisis to show up. Visit them instead, when things are really good, and use that time to patiently build a connection with your clients so that when things go south, you will have a reserve of goodwill to fall back on.

There are other reasons why you should see your clients face-to-face. Email is two-dimensional. Communication is three-dimensional, meaning that when you sit across a desk, a conference table, or seats at a restaurant, you get to see all the messages left unsaid. You can take your cues from body posture, hand gestures, facial expressions, and voice inflections; all things missing from an email. They can be the difference between getting it, and not getting it.

Could you default to a phone call instead of making a house call? Yes, the phone will at least make you privy to how a client is speaking—if you listen carefully, you can hear frustration, confusion, and, of course, anger—but compare the limited virtues of a phone call with the nearly boundless virtues of face-to-face. A telephone call should be your last resort. An in-person visit should be your preferred, first option.

I recall sitting at a speech given by noted author Simon Sinek. There came a moment when Simon said, "Business is human."

Nothing quite matches Simon's simple, elegant, and utterly profound assertion that *business is human*, by pointing out that no matter how much technology advances the cause of marketing, there is not, nor will there ever be, a replacement for face-to-face, in-person connections with clients and colleagues.

So get on that plane, on that train, or in that automobile, and go see your clients.

FOLLOW UP

If showing up is important, then following up is even more essential to the success and vitality of your client relationships. It seems so obvious: a client calls, you call back. A client emails. You email or call back. But something weird happens along the way: *you don't do it*, or if you do it, it gets done hours or days later, rendering the response nearly useless.

This is a rule with exceptions limited to true emergencies; otherwise, the goal is to respond within an hour, or two at most, of receiving an overture from a client. If you're in a meeting, connect on a break. If the matter is truly urgent, excuse yourself from the room, find a hallway, and call back.

If you're on a plane, connect before taking off or immediately upon landing. If there's reason and the airline you're flying on offers it, and if your flight is long enough, buy their Wi-Fi access, giving you the ability to be in contact throughout your flight.

Check your email and voicemail in the morning, before you leave for work. Check them again, in the evening. If a client is in touch, get back in touch with them.

Most clients I know *hate* radio silence. They feel ignored, neglected, and overlooked. Over time, this lack of responsiveness takes a toll. It undermines your relationship and erodes trust.

Being in touch does not necessarily require you to have the answer. It *does* require you to acknowledge a client question or request. The most important thing for you to say is, "*I got your voicemail (or email). I'm on the case, and I'll get back to you with an answer by day's end*" (or whatever time you're committing yourself to).

Now the dark side of this is you can never escape the laser-like focus of your client's needs. They might call you late at night, early in the morning, on weekends and holidays. Is there no rest for the weary and overstressed?

There is. If constant contact becomes a problem, work out a system with your clients by agreeing on what constitutes an emergency that requires an immediate response, and what doesn't. Agree on rules about what's fair and reasonable. A call on a Saturday at 3:00 A.M. about an issue that can wait until Monday is not reasonable.

But if I'm on vacation and disaster strikes back at my agency, would I prefer to remain blissfully unaware, only to face a meltdown on my return, or would I prefer to know about the issue, so I can attempt to resolve it while I'm away?

For me, this is a rhetorical question. I hope the same is true for you.

Okay, that's client follow-up. What about colleague follow-up?

As important as it is to follow up with clients, it is equally important to follow up with colleagues. Advertising and marketing is by its nature a collaborative venture. Problems get solved in a collaborative culture, given everyone works together to solve them. So why are there so many problems that remain stubbornly unresolved, and why do the same problems occur again and again?

It was Albert Einstein who said, "Insanity is doing the same thing over and over again and expecting different results."

You solve problems by following up with one another, sharing with one another, and making sure the problem you committed to resolve doesn't get replicated by someone else. That's the best way to avoid insanity.

Your enemy, if there is one, is your competitors, and you should focus outwardly on them. To do that, you need to focus inwardly on follow-up and become really good at it.

━━━━━

SPEAK UP

Speak up is shorthand for communicating, orally or in writing, in groups large and small, in settings both formal and informal.

As I mentioned earlier in this book, account people are commercial writers, and by this I do not mean writers of commercials, a domain appropriately reserved for a firm's creative copywriters. Commercial writing is a presentation, a letter of proposal, a point-of-view positioning, a conference report, emails of every stripe, virtually anything that is committed to paper, real or digital.

I confess I can't make you better writers—this is a challenge way beyond my pay grade—but I can recommend three books that can, two of which appeared in the previous edition of, *The Art of Client Service*. Yes, I am being redundant, but for good cause.

The first is the most famous of the lot: William Strunk and E.B. White's brilliant, short, timeless classic, *The Elements of Style*. On my shelf is a relatively current fourth edition, with Roger Angell supplementing the introduction of his stepfather, E.B. White, with a forward of his own.

Also on my shelf is the third edition, purchased years ago, in 1979. Little has changed, and little should, and there's a reason why *The Elements of Style* remains the number one writing skills bestseller on Amazon. There is no better reference you can use to help make your writing sharper, clearer, and more concise.

William Zinser's *On Writing Well* is nearly a match for *The Elements of Style* in its concision, clarity, and utility. Now in its thirtieth anniversary edition, it, too, has stood the test of time.

A more recent book is by former Ogilvy & Mather Chairman Ken Roman, called *Writing that Works*. It has the advantage of being writing by someone who knows first-hand what it means to be an advertising account person, and covers all forms of commercial writing account people use to ply their trade.

This trio of books will surely advance the cause of clear communication, should you choose to invest in them and follow their precepts and guidelines. But the best way to become a better writer is to write more. There are some skills driven by talent. There are some skills driven by instinct. Writing is a skill driven by practice. The more you do it, the better you will become.

While I'm on the subject of confessions, let me make another one: just as I cannot make you better writers, I am equally unable to make you better speakers. But I have some books to recommend and some advice to share, which I hope you will find helpful.

There comes a point in the workshops I give when I ask those in attendance if they ever have to speak in public, either in the form of a formal presentation, or in a more offhand, spur-of-the-moment, casual way. Inevitably, just about every hand in the room will go up.

I then ask, "How many of you are afraid?"

Only a few hands go up, but one of the hands that elevates is mine. My point is simple: if people tell you they are not afraid to speak before a group, they either are lying to you, or lying to themselves.

This is one of the points Scott Berkun makes in a book I recommend, *Confessions of a Public Speaker*. Berkun claims that people are more afraid of public speaking than they are of dying. Think about this for a moment—think about all the major actors, musicians, and other performers who suffer from stage fright—and you'll quickly see why it is so hard to be good at this. And yet to be great at client service, you need to be effective and confident in front of an audience.

Berkun's book is helpful, if for no other reason than it is good to hear about someone else's travails in front of audiences, but to his book I would add a second, written by former television news anchor and now consultant Suzanne Bates, called *Speak Like a CEO*.

Title aside—I know a fair number of CEOs who are just god-awful as public speakers, and not the kind of people you want to emulate—the book is a very practical guide to get better at what many of us find terrifying: standing at the front of a room and commanding it.

To these two books I would add three pieces of advice:

- **Begin at the end**, meaning when you walk into a room, you want to know what you want the outcome to be. It could simply be another meeting, where you continue the conversation. It could be a request for a proposal, where you are asked to take the next step in the process of converting a prospect into a client. It could be to solve a problem or preempt one. It could be to prevail in a competitive new business initiative.

Whatever the desired outcome, know what it is at the outset, and build whatever you are sharing to achieve this one, and I mean only one, objective.

- **Know the three things you want to communicate**. If you enter a room with a long list of things you want to get across, chances are you will succeed at none of them. In fact, the longer your list, the less effective you will be.

  My suggestion is that you make your list short—three items at most—and dedicate yourself to accomplishing them.

- **Rehearse, then rehearse again**. There's a very old joke that goes, "Question: how do you get to Carnegie Hall? Answer: practice." Like writing, where the more you do it, the better you will become, your ability as a speaker increases the more you rehearse. And the more you rehearse, the more confident and conversational your delivery will be.

As much as you might think that writers are the domain of the creative department, and speaking in public is primarily the responsibility of people more senior, practiced, and accomplished than you are, the reality is, the more effective you are at communicating, the more likely your career as a client service person will benefit.

To put it simply: if you want to be great at client service, you need to become great at speaking up.

MAKE IT UP

One clear insight is worth a thousand data points, and ideas are where you find them, but the key to making it up is being open to exploring far and wide in search of a solution or an inspiration.

Insights often come in a flash of recognition. I've already written about Occam's Razor and the importance of simple, the value of a perfectly framed question, the power of observation, the need to master your craft, and being open to serendipity. These are five techniques that can help you be more creative.

NEVER GIVE UP

Advertising and marketing agencies typically have a high fatality rate, meaning they lose clients far more frequently than you might expect, creating turmoil and uncertainty among those who work in the business. You would think this loss of business is due to client dissatisfaction with strategy, or a lack of ideas. That can be the case, but it is just as likely clients become frustrated with things that go wrong that shouldn't.

A budget that's wrong. A schedule that's off. A call or email that doesn't get returned promptly. Communication that's unclear. Help that is not forthcoming.

I wrote about this earlier, and I'm writing about it again to make a point: it's hard to get a strategy right; it's even harder to formulate ideas that work. But these other tasks? Client service people *should* get them right, and when they don't, it should come as no surprise when clients become disillusioned, angry, or even worse, so dissatisfied they seek another agency.

Great client service people do not let this happen. They stay after every task, making sure they get it right. They deal with each client democratically, not distinguishing between accounts large and small, people kind or unkind, assignments easy or hard. Everyone they work with gets their full and undivided attention. All clients are made to feel as if they are the only client.

Great client service people care about what they do, and the ones who do it the best never give up. They are the ones who perform beyond category. What does this mean?

Most everyone knows the premier event in professional road racing is the Tour de France. From the Tour de France, I know that each of the hills the competitors ascend and descend is rated from one—the hardest—through four—the easiest—based mostly on each climb's steepness and length. Hills that are harder than category one are rated "beyond category." Those who are able to scale such climbs are said to perform beyond category.

That's cycling. What about serving clients? What does it mean to perform beyond category in advertising?

This is not about doing the obvious, expected, or so-called easy stuff in client service. It's about doing the less obvious, unexpected, harder stuff. The stuff that challenges you, pushes you to be better, demands you to try, and try again, in the face of failure.

In your career you will face challenges that range from four—relatively easy to address—to one—incredibly hard to address. I do not know how these challenges will unfold—they will differ in scope and complexity largely based on your circumstances. But if history is a window of prediction, they likely will be about time, money, the work, or the relationship. If they reside in one of these categories, I hope the pages of this book have helped equip you to address them just a bit more effectively.

There also will be moments when you are tested beyond category. When that day comes, I am confident you will be equal to the task.

ACKNOWLEDGMENTS:
REMEMBER TO SAY "THANK YOU"

In the summer of 2015, my then-agent, Jim Donovan, received an email from my then-publisher, Kaplan, with this: "Analysis of your recent royalty statements indicates that it would be appropriate for us to revert publication rights for all formats to you."

After two editions and 11 printings, Kaplan was saying goodbye. Okay, I can deal with this, I thought. But this required I find not just a new publisher, but also a new agent, given that Jim was no longer representing books like mine.

I did both, starting with my convincing Jeff Herman I was worthy of his representation. Jeff, to his credit and for which I am extraordinarily grateful, managed to attract the attention of editor Richard Narramore at John Wiley & Sons. It was refreshing to have an editor again, someone with a track record—Richard's authors include Luke Sullivan (*Hey Whipple, Squeeze This*) and Jon Steele (*Truth, Lies & Advertising*). Credit goes to Richard, first for supporting this book, and second, for challenging me to make it better.

Credit also goes to Bel Downey, for the whimsical and well-crafted cover that graces this book. Many thanks for your patience and perseverance, Bel.

I have been in this business longer than I care to admit, and so much of what is contained in this book was prompted or inspired by a client, a colleague, or friend. There were the people who wrote or emailed me, and those who asked questions or made astute observations in my presentations, workshops, and speeches. All added to my knowledge, understanding, and when I was smart enough, insight.

It would be a fool's errand to try to list all the people who truly mattered as I wrote this; you know who you are, and I'm hoping all of you can accept my heartfelt appreciation for your contributions large and small. There are, however, three people who are worthy of special mention.

The first is my dad, who was an entrepreneur and a salesman, who taught me, among many other things, that it is okay to make mistakes. I still recall wrecking his car in a parking lot, being incredibly afraid to tell him, only to have him surprise me by saying, "You're new to driving; of course you're going to break things. We'll get this fixed, and let me show you how next time you can avoid wrapping the car around a pole."

There must be a thousand clients and colleagues whose counsel I value—Mary Stibal, Kim Carpenter, Sallyann Colonna, Vivian Young, Phil Palazzo, and Lisa Lefebvre, among countless others—but the one individual who taught me the most about what it means to be in advertising is the second person on my list of three, Mike Slosberg, who never gave up on me, even when I surely deserved being abandoned. Mike has forgotten more than I will ever know about advertising, but he was kind enough and patient enough to share some of his wisdom with me.

The third and by far the most important person in my life is, in addition to being my COO, CFO, and CTO, my partner, best friend, and confidante, my wife Roberta.

Without you, honey, this book would not be.

POSTSCRIPT

DRESSING THE PART

Early in my career, I worked for a very smart, very personable, and outrageously funny executive. He was a big guy, kind of a bowling ball with legs. A client described him as "an unmade waterbed." That moniker captured his rumpled, shirttail-out, tie-askew style.

He could pull this off because of his outsized personality and big brain. It wouldn't work for most other people, and even if it did, I wouldn't recommend it.

That's because you are the agency's lead representative to your client, the manifestation of the agency's brand and culture. So regardless if the style you cultivate is Chicago conservative, New York downtown hip, or San Francisco laid-back, grooming counts. It affects how others see you and how they judge you professionally. It can affect how you feel about yourself.

Dressing the part used to be easy. With the exception of the creative department, where style could run amok with little fear of reprisal, men defaulted to sober suits and ties; women did much the same. In the era of casual dress, this has become vastly harder to decode, and those of us in the business might find ourselves not resorting to a standard uniform, but instead calibrating what we wear to the client and the occasion. Do I wear a suit? Do I dress casual? And what, exactly, is meant by *casual*?

This means redoubling your efforts to get the styling details right, starting with a decent haircut, ending with a decent pair of shoes, and navigating everything in between. It's more about investing time and attention than dollars and cents. It's a matter of taste. I know guys who wear expensive suits and still manage to look disheveled. I know other guys who wear a sport shirt and jeans and look completely pulled together. I know women who spend a fortune on clothes but don't get the look right. I know other women who bargain basement shop and look terrific.

Your agency probably has a style; it might even have a dress code, written or unwritten, but widely understood. If this is the case, take your cues from what you see or what the rules say. If not, here are a few suggestions.

- If you're meeting with a client, adapt the client's dress code. For example, if your client considers "casual" to be khakis and polos, you can do the same, but take it up a notch. Put on a dress shirt, add a sport coat, abandon the running shoes for a great pair of loafers. Accessorize with a cool watch and a good briefcase. Women can wear a blouse and skirt, a sweater and slacks, or anything else a level above casual, instead of a suit.

- Casual *is not code for slovenly.* If you're not meeting with clients and the agency is a dress-casual place, then dress casually, but don't take casual too far. Plus, keep a dress shirt or blouse in your office, in case you have to meet with a client unexpectedly.

- *You can push casual a bit further in the summer.* When it's really hot, get rid of the jacket, unless you have to have one to meet with your client.

- *Wear a suit, but dress it down a bit.* No tie. Maybe a sport shirt or sweater rather than a dress shirt or blouse. Hipper shoes rather than wingtips or pumps.

- *Suede is great.* If you wear leather shoes, you have to keep them polished. Suede shoes take a minute to brush; no polishing required.

- *Invest in a few suits that are the best you can afford.* It's better to have a few well-tailored items than more options of lower quality. They will fit you better and will last longer. That means staying away from trendy, highly perishable designs, fabrics, and patterns, and gravitating instead toward classic design in muted fabrics and patterns. If you get bored with the same three or four suits in your wardrobe, don't buy another suit. Buy a new shirt or tie, or blouse, to change the look.

- *If your client is out of town, or if you have to travel, buy clothes that travel.* For example, in suits, crepe wool is great. It holds its shape, resists wrinkles, and packs well. In the age of carry-on, the last thing you want to do is check a bag, so wear that suit jacket or sport coat, rather than exiling it to the land of rumpled and ruined by packing it. If you are going to be on the road for multiple days, you can change the look without needing to change jackets by varying shirts, ties, vests, and the like.

- *Ask for style help if you need it.* Take a long look in the mirror. If you don't have what it takes to style yourself, admit it, and find some help. I have a colleague in the business who always looks great. He didn't have a clue on how to dress, but he was smart enough to enlist the help of a friend who did. Now he never shops alone.

- *Think in terms of a uniform.* Men have done this for years, and so have some women I know. For men, the uniform used to be a pinstripe suit, white shirt, striped tie, wingtip shoes. That's not the uniform I'd suggest for most agency people, but the concept makes sense. A uniform allows you to mix and match various pieces in your wardrobe. It allows you to work with fewer items, which allows you to invest a little more in each piece. It makes packing for travel easier. Lots of New Yorkers have made black their uniform color. They can get dressed in the dark. Not that black isn't cool, but you don't have to be quite so strict, or so somber. Confining your business wardrobe to just a few colors—black, blue, and gray, for example—does make dressing easier.

Style won't make or break your career. There are dozens of successful account people who don't have a clue about fashion. There are others who know how to dress, but that's all they know (the classic "empty suit"). Still, it's a competitive world, and you need every edge you can get. Looking good is just one more detail in a business that is all about details. So why not get this one right? It just might make a difference.

A BUNCH OF BOOKS TO MAKE YOU BETTER AT WHAT YOU DO

As hard as this is to believe, it was more than 13 years ago that I first compiled a list of 15 books that every account person should read. Back then, I asked myself, "Will these books endure?" At the time, I had no idea I would be sitting down today to revisit the list to see what I could discard and what I could add.

The good news: all but one of the books continue to pass the endurance test. In fairness, some—like David Ogilvy's or Strunk and White's—received high scores well before I recommended them. Other books, like Malcolm Gladwell's *The Tipping Point,* or Tom Monahan's *The Do-It-Yourself Lobotomy,* have proven their worth over time. The only book that fails the test is Ron Hoff's *I Can See You Naked.* Frankly, I never was entirely comfortable with recommending that book, but at the time there were few books of merit on public speaking. I've addressed this by replacing Hoff's book with Suzanne Bates's *Speak Like a CEO,* which struck me as loaded with incredibly practical advice on how to get better in front of an audience.

The bad news: there continue to be way too many books! In the past four years, I don't know how many hundreds of titles have appeared on the market, many of them truly worthy of inclusion. But my initial goal remains: to give you a short list of books, not an interminable one.

For the second edition of *The Art of Client Service,* I selected five books to add to my earlier list of 15. The selection is admittedly imperfect, and I'm certain you could do as well or better with your own picks. I've kept all five, but integrated them into the original list of 15, making the total now 20.

For this new edition, I've added five new books, so now there are 25 titles on the combined list, extending over three editions of *The Art of Client Service*.

In no particular order, here are my five latest choices:

1. Malcolm Gladwell made the first list with his book, *The Tipping Point*. He made the second list with, *Blink*. He makes this third list with *David and Goliath*, a book worth reading for just its opening chapter about the biblical David as an ostensible underdog (spoiler: he's not).

2. Adam Grant broke new ground with *Give and Take*. In a world gone cynical, he makes a compelling case for how being a giver trumps being a taker in achieving career success.

3. You wouldn't expect a book by a restaurateur to make the list, but Danny Meyer's *Setting the Table* is one of the best books I've read on serving clients well.

4. I knew Simon Sinek before he became famous, when he was a young planner at Messner Vetere Berger McNamee Schmetter/EuroRSCG, before he wrote *Start With Why,* and then later, *Leaders Eat Last*. He was smart then; he's smart now. If you want proof, watch one of his TED talks.

5. If you need to laugh, read Scott Berkun's *Confessions of a Public Speaker;* it's honest and funny, about a skill all of us need to get better at.

So there you have it: five new books to add to the list of 20.

ON COMMUNICATING

1. Strunk, William, and E. B. White. *The Elements of Style,* 4th ed. Boston: Allyn & Bacon, 2000.

2. Zinsser, William. *On Writing Well,* 6th ed. New York: HarperPerennial, 1998.

3. Roman, Kenneth, and Joel Raphaelson. *Writing That Works.* New York: Quill/HarperCollins, 2000.

4. Bates, Suzanne. *How to Speak Like a CEO.* New York: McGraw-Hill, 2005.

ON CLIENT RELATIONSHIPS

5. Maister, David H., Charles H. Green, and Robert M. Galford. *The Trusted Advisor.* New York: Free Press, 2000.

6. Sheth, Jagdish, and Andrew Sobel. *Clients for Life.* New York: Simon & Schuster, 2000.

7. Solomon, Robert. *The Art of Client Service,* 3rd ed. Hoboken, NJ: John Wiley & Sons, 2016.

ON CREATIVITY AND ADVERTISING

8. Monahan, Tom. *The Do-It-Yourself Lobotomy.* New York: John Wiley & Sons, 2002.

9. Sullivan, Luke. *Hey Whipple, Squeeze This.* New York: John Wiley & Sons, 1998.

10. Ogilvy, David. *Ogilvy on Advertising.* New York: Vintage Books, 1985.

11. Fallon, Pat, and Fed Senn. *Juicing the Orange.* Boston: Harvard Business School Press, 2006.

12. Kelley, Tom, and Jonathan Littman. *The Art of Innovation.* New York: Doubleday, 2001.

13. Neumeier, Marty. *The Brand Gap: How to Bridge the Distance Between Business Strategy and Design.* Indianapolis, IN: New Riders, 2006.

ON STRATEGY

14. Ries, Al, and Jack Trout. *Positioning: The Battle for Your Mind*. New York: McGraw-Hill Trade, 2000.

15. Morgan, Adam. *Eating the Big Fish*. New York: John Wiley & Sons, 1999.

16. Steel, Jon. *Truth, Lies, and Advertising*. New York: John Wiley & Sons, 1998.

17. Gladwell, Malcolm. *The Tipping Point*. Boston: Little, Brown and Company, 2000.

18. Gladwell, Malcolm. *Blink: The Power of Thinking Without Thinking*. Boston: Little, Brown and Company, 2005.

19. Verklin, David, and Bernice Kanner. *Watch This, Listen Up, Click Here*. Hoboken, NJ: John Wiley & Sons, 2007.

ON BUSINESS LEADERSHIP

20. Collins, Jim. *Good to Great*. New York: HarperBusiness, 2001.

FIVE NEW BOOKS

21. Gladwell, Malcolm. *David and Goliath*. Brown: Little, Brown and Company, 2013.

22. Grant, Adam. *Give and Take*. New York: Viking, 2013.

23. Meyer, Danny. *Setting the Table*. New York: HarperCollins, 2006.

24. Sinek, Simon. *Leaders Eat Last*. New York: Portfolio, 2014.

25. Berkun, Scott. *Confessions of a Public Speaker*. Sebastopol, CA: O'Reilly Media, 2011.

ABOUT THE AUTHOR

Trained as a direct marketer who embraced Digital early on, Robert Solomon is known for his expertise as a brand strategist and new business developer. He also is a commercial writer, published author, and expert speaker and workshop leader, who also is certified as an organizational and executive coach, particularly skilled in job search.

As varied as these disciplines are, they share a single objective: they are about changing behavior of a company, a client, an employer, or a consumer.

Robert runs Solomon Strategic, a firm he founded in 1999 to provide marketing counsel to advertising agencies, client companies, and individual marketing professionals.

Robert has handled a wide range of consulting assignments, in both offline and online media, for more than a score of clients, including Ammirati Puris Lintas, Blitz, BoomBox, Brandmuscle, Chase Insurance, Cognitive Arts, Condé Nast, Digitas Health Lifebrands, Deep Focus, Draft Worldwide, Ferrara and Company, Initiative Media North America, PALAZZO | Investment Bankers, Procurian, R/GA Interactive, Saatchi and Saatchi X, Sotheby's, and Womenkind.

Robert previously was President and CEO of Rapp Collins New York, President of Direct and Interactive Marketing at Ammirati Puris Lintas, General Manager of FCB Direct West, and Senior Vice President of Bronner Slosberg Humphrey (now Digitas).

Robert lives in Napa, California, with his wife Roberta and with the world's best dogs, Alvin and Molly.

INDEX